George Brett

From Here to
Cooperstown

By
no.5
George Brett

with Steve Cameron

NATIONAL ASSOCIATION OF PROFESSIONAL BASEBALL LEAGUES

IMPORTANT NOTICE

The attention of both Club and Player is specifically directed to the following excerpts from Professional Baseball Rule 3 (a):

"No Club shall make a contract different from the uniform contract and no club shall make a contract containing non-reserve clause, except permission be first secured from the . . . President of the National Association. The making of any agreement between a Club and Player not embodied in the contract shall subject both parties to discipline."

Uniform Player Contract

The BILLINGS BASEBALL CLUB .... Club, herein called the Club, a member of the ....,
PIONEER .... League, "Association" and .... GEORGE HOWARD BRETT
628 Penn street, El Segundo, California (90245)

herein called the player, of........

Parties

Recital The League of which the Club is a member is a leagu.... ....tion of Professional Baseball Leagues
(hereinafter referred to as the "National Association". As suc.... ....its League, it is a party to the Na-
Constitution and By-Laws of the League of which it is a mem.... .....Agreement of the Na-
tional Association of Professional Baseball Leagues (hereinaft.... .....ent"), and the
Professional Baseball Agreement and Rules, between the Na.... .....League of
Professional Baseball Clubs and its constituent clubs and the.... .....
clubs, on the other hand. The purpose of these Agreement.... .....
some professional baseball by defining the relations betw.... .....
League, and by vesting in a designated Commissioner of.... .....
Association and in the League President, broad powers of....

In consideration of the facts above recited and of....

Agreement Employment 1. The Club hereby employs the Pl....
....led services as a baseball player in c....
YEAR▶ $ 71 , including the Club's training season, th....
19 which the Club may participate, and in any game or....
Player covenants that at the time he signs this contra....
other than the one party to this contract and that he....
service stated and such other duties as may be requi....

Payment 500.00 (five hundred dollars p....
$........ In semi-monthly installments, after the c....
is "abroad", in which event the amount then d....
return "home" of the Club. The terms "home"....
has its baseball park.
The obligation to make such payment....
quent date as the Player's service may comme.... ....
official league play-off series in which the C....
the playing season only, he shall receive s....
employment in any month bears to the number of....

Photo: Brothers and teammates in the minors, Bobby (l) and George.

Loyalty 3. (a) The Player agrees to serve diligently and faithfull.... ....
assigned, as provided in paragraph 6 hereof; to keep himself in first-cla.... ....
all requirements of the Club respecting conduct and service of its team and its p.... ....
and pledges himself to the public to conform to high standards of personal conduct, fair p....

(b) In addition to his service in connection with the active playing of baseball, the Player agree....
Club and participate in any and all promotional activities of the Club and its League, which, in the opinion o....
promote the welfare of the Club or Professional Baseball.

Baseball Promotion (c) The Player agrees that, while in the Club's uniform, photographs, whether still or action, and motion pictures may
be taken and telecasts made, of himself, individually or with others, at such times or places as the Club may designate; that
all rights therein shall belong to the Club; and that they may be used, reproduced or otherwise disseminated by the Club, directly or indirectly, in any manner the Club desires. The Player further agrees that during the playing season (as defined in
paragraph 1 of this contract) he will not make public appearances, participate in radio or television programs, permit his
picture to be taken, sponsor commercial products or services, or write or sponsor newspaper or magazine articles, without

Pictures in each case the written consent of his Club, which, however, shall not be withheld except in the reasonable interests of the
Club or Professional Baseball, provided, however, that at no time shall the Player, while in the Club's uniform, engage in any
of the foregoing activities without the written consent of the Club.

4. (a) The Player represents that he has no physical or mental defects known to him, which would prevent or impair
performance of his services.
(b) The Player represents that he does not, directly or indirectly, own stock or have any financial interest in the
ownership or earnings of any Major League or National Association Club, except as hereinafter expressly set forth, and
covenants that he will not hereafter, while under contract to the Club, or any assignee thereof, acquire or hold any such stock
or interest, except in accordance with Professional Baseball Rule 20 (e).

5. (a) The Player agrees that, while under contract and prior to expiration of the Club's right to renew the contract,
and until he reports to his Club for spring training, if this contract is renewed, for the purpose of avoiding injuries he will not
Playing for Others play baseball otherwise than for the Club, except that he may participate in post-season games as prescribed in the National
Association Agreement.

(b) The Player and the Club recognize and agree that the Player's participation in other sports may impair or destroy
his ability and skill as a baseball player. Accordingly, the Player agrees he will not engage in professional football, basketball, hockey or

Other ....and that, except with the written consent of the Club, he will not play professional football....

PAGE TWO

6. (a) The Playe.... agrees that this contract may be assigned....
other Club in accordance with the Professional Baseball Rules and Nat....
(b) No assignment of this contract shall be made to a Club o....
season unless the compensation to be paid by the assignee Club is at le....
hereof.
If an assignment of this contract is made to a Club of lower cla....
not less than the rate usually paid by the assignee Club to its players of....
a Club commonly owned or controlled by the assignor. A subsequent retr....
son or thereafter shall not entitle the Player to be paid any difference....
transfer.
(c) The Player shall report to the assignee Club promptly (as provid....
of written or telegraphic notice from the Club of the assignment. If the P....
any payment for the period from the date he received written or telegraphic....
the assignee Club.
(d) Upon such assignment, the assignee Club shall be liable to the Play....
....eports to, and contracts with, the assignee Club, and the assignor Club su....
....rued at date of.... .... assignment plus (if he so reports) payment for the trav....

....s in this contract to the "Club" shall be deemed to mean....
....lub is in arrears to the Player for any payments due him u....
....more than fifteen (15) days to perform any other obligation....
....be entitled to apply to the President of the National Assoc....
....y such default as to such payment or other obligation with....
....this contract by a declaration of free agency, but the Clu....
....date of such termination.
....termine this contract upon written or telegraphic notice to th....
....neglect to conform his personal conduct to standards of good....
....ass physical condition, or to obey the Club's requirements res....
....nion of the Club's management, to exhibit sufficient skill or co....
....s team; or
....neglect to render his services hereunder, or in any other mann....
....also terminate this contract as provided in Regulation 2 on Pag....
.... disability resulting directly from injury sustained in the course....
....te of such injury has been given by the Player, as provided in sai....
....benefits set forth in said Regulation.
....ating this contract in accordance with sub-paragraphs (b) or (c....
....des of its League applicable thereto.
....he Club accept as part of this contract the Regulations printed o....
....the Player agree to accept, abide by and comply with all provision....
....Club is a member, of the Professional Baseball Rules, and of the....
....duct and player-club relations, and with all decisions of the C....
....National Association, and of the League President pursuant there....

....March 1 (or if a Sunday then the next succeeding business d....
....contract, the Club may notify the Player of its intention to rene....
....year, except that the compensation rate shall be such as the pa....
....ave been made it the contract is delivered to the player person....
....Club, or his address following his signature hereto, which shal....
....have been notified by the Player, through registered mail, of his....
....compensation rate shall be determined as provided in paragraph....
....compensation rate fixed by the Club or else will not play otherw....
....renew this contract as provided in sub-paragraph (a) of this p....
....the Player have been taken into consideration in determining th....

....ute between the Player and the Club arising under the provisio....
....the National Association, as an arbitrator, and the arbitrator....
....right of appeal as is set forth in Regulation 8 on Page Four....
....dent, the President and Executive Committee of the Nationa....
....public the findings, decision and record of any inquiry, inve....
....evidence or information, given, received or obtained in con....
....Federal or State legislation, regulations, executive or oth....
....effect, which may directly or indirectly affect the Playe....
....or the Executive Committee of the National Associatio....

....sident of the National Association", "Executive Com....
....mean the person or persons holding any such office or e....
....during the term of this contract or any renewal thereof.
....to receive or has received any additional paymen....
....urce whatsoever in connection with th....

...yer is to receive a bonus of 25,000.00 (twenty-five thousand dollars)
...able upon approval of this contract by the President of the National
...lation, as follows:

1.) 15,000.00 (fifteen thousand dollars) upon approval.
2.) 10,000.00 (ten thousand dollars) January 15, 1972

...ayer is to participate in the Incentive Bonus Plan, copy of plan is
...ing furnished the player

...ayer is to participate in the College Scholorship Plan for (8)eight
...emesters not to exceed 1,000.00 (one thousand dollars) per semester.Copy
...f the plan is being furnished the player.

...Player is guaranteed return transportation (via air-coach) to the players
...home at the close of the season.

15. (a) Any provision of this contract which entitled the Player to receive a bonus payment if he is retained by the Club on a designated date or for a designated period shall be subject to the following: In the event of the Player's placement on the Restricted, Voluntarily Retired, Military, Disqualified or Ineligible List, prior to the date upon which the bonus payment becomes due, payment of the bonus shall be suspended until after the Player has been reinstated to the Active List and has reported to and been retained by the Club for the number of days equal to and complying with the conditions of this contract; provided, however, that in case of placement on the Military List no contingently postponed bonus payment shall become due until after the Player, following reinstatement, has reported to the Club (or an assignee thereof) and been retained on the Active List for at least 16 days of a playing season or seasons.

(b) Any provision in this contract which entitled the Player to receive a deferred bonus payment, or payments, on a designated date, or dates, shall be subject to the following: In the event of the Player's placement on the Restricted, Voluntarily Retired, Disqualified or Ineligible List prior to the date upon which such payment, or any installment thereof, becomes due, the Club shall further defer any such payment or payments until after the Player has reported to the Club following reinstatement from such inactive list and the date the deferred payment or any installment thereof would otherwise become due. In the event of the Player's placement on the Military List, the foregoing shall apply in all particulars, except that if the Player's placement on such inactive list and the date the deferred payment or other incapacitation while in the Armed Forces death occurs while he is in the Armed Forces or if he suffers an injury or other incapacitation while in the Armed Forces which renders him permanently incapable of playing professional baseball, the deferred bonus payment, or payments, shall be made to his estate, in the event of such death, or to him, in the event of such permanent incapacitation.

(c) In the event the official date of placement on any of the inactive lists enumerated above is later than the date the Player ceased to be an active player, the earlier date shall apply in determining the new date of the contingent and/or deferred bonus following the Player's reinstatement to the Active List of his Club.

16. The Club and the Player covenant that this contract fully sets forth all understandings and agreements between them, and agree that no understandings or agreements, whether heretofore or hereafter made, shall be valid, recognized, or be of any effect whatsoever, unless and until set forth in a new Uniform Player Contract executed by Player and Club, filed with and approved by the President of the National Association and complying with the Professional Baseball Rules and National Association Agreement.

This contract shall not be valid or effective unless filed with and approved by the President of the National Association.

This contract shall be delivered to the Player, in person, or by registered or certified mail.

A copy of this contract when executed must be delivered to the Player, in person, or by registered or certified mail.

.... A.D., 19..71.

Signed this .....25..... day of .....June.....

By ....
Authorized Club Official Sign Here

.....Bellingham..... (Club)

This contract must be received at National Association office within 20 days from date it is signed by Player.
Player MUST DATE AND SIGN IN OWN HANDWRITING, giving initials and Street and HOME CITY address.

.... (Month) .... , A.D., 19.71.

Signed this .....30th..... (Date) ..... day of .....June.....
Player date here in OWN handwriting at time of signing this contract.

Consent of Parent or Guardian
Consent is given to execution of this contract by the minor player party hereto and such consent shall be effective as to any assignment or renewal thereof under Paragraphs 6 and 10 hereof.

.....John H. Brett..... Parent-Guardian.

PLAYER SIGN HERE
.....George Howard Brett.....

Player's Home Address — Street and No.
.....628 Penn St.....

City and State
.....El Segundo California.....
.....90245.....

"Looking back, the thing that has amazed me the most about George and his baseball career is that here was a very good high school player, who many so-called experts thought was the third best player on his high school team.

At every level in the minor leagues he looked like he was in a little bit over his head early in the season. But, by the end of each season he improved dramatically in all facets of the game, not just physically but more importantly, his mental approach to the game and the way he went about his work.

As his brother, I have had the opportunity to observe many good qualities in George, his determination, his focus. Most importantly, George was a good listener. He listened to his mentors. He had many along the road, from his roots in El Segundo to his adopted home of Kansas City.

Now that George, the youngest of the four Brett brothers, is going to the Hall of Fame, I hope that when he pinches himself he'll realize that his baseball career was not just a dream. It really did happen and his dream did come true."

-Bobby Brett

Published by Addax Publishing Group, Inc.
Copyright © 1999 by George Brett

All rights reserved. No part of this book may be reproduced or transmitted in any form or by any means, electronic or mechanical, including photocopying, recording, or by any information storage and retrieval system, without the written permission of the Publisher.
For Information address:
Addax Publishing Group, Inc.
8643 Hauser Drive, Suite 235, Lenexa, KS 66215

Bob Snodgrass
Publisher

Jerry Hirt
Art Direction/Design

Nelson Elliott
Managing Editor

Darcie Kidson
Publicity

Development assistance: Michelle Zwickle-Washington, Sharon Snodgrass,
An Beard, Gary Carson

ISBN: 1-886110-79-4

Distributed to the trade by Andrews McMeel Publishing
4520 Main Street
Kansas City, MO 64111

Printed in the USA

3 5 7 9 10 8 6 4 2

ATTENTION: SCHOOLS AND BUSINESSES
Addax Publishing Group, Inc. books are available at quantity discounts with bulk purchase for education, business, or sales promotional use. For information, please write to: Special Sales Department, Addax Publishing Group, 8643 Hauser Drive, Suite 235, Lenexa, Kansas 66215

Library of Congress Cataloging in Publication Data

Brett, George.
George Brett : from here to Cooperstown / by George Brett with
Steve Cameron.
p. cm.
ISBN 1-886110-79-4 (hc)
1. Brett, George. 2. Baseball players--United States Biography.
3. Kansas City Royals (Baseball team) 4. Brett, George Pictorial
works. 5. Baseball players--United States Pictorial works.
6. Kansas City Royals (Baseball team) Pictorial works. I. Cameron
Steve. II. Title.
GV865.B715A3 1999
796.357'092--dc21

99-22888
CIP

[B]

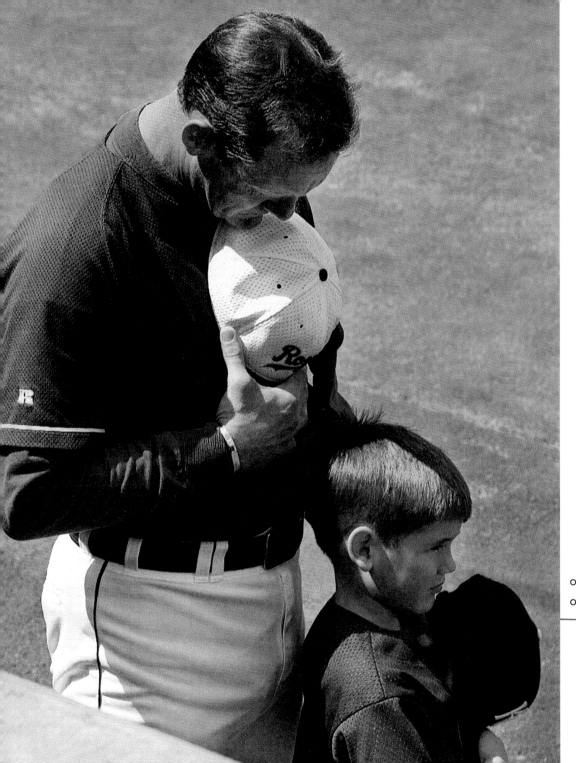

George and son Jackson pause for a moment of silence during 1999 spring training in memory of Joe DiMaggio.

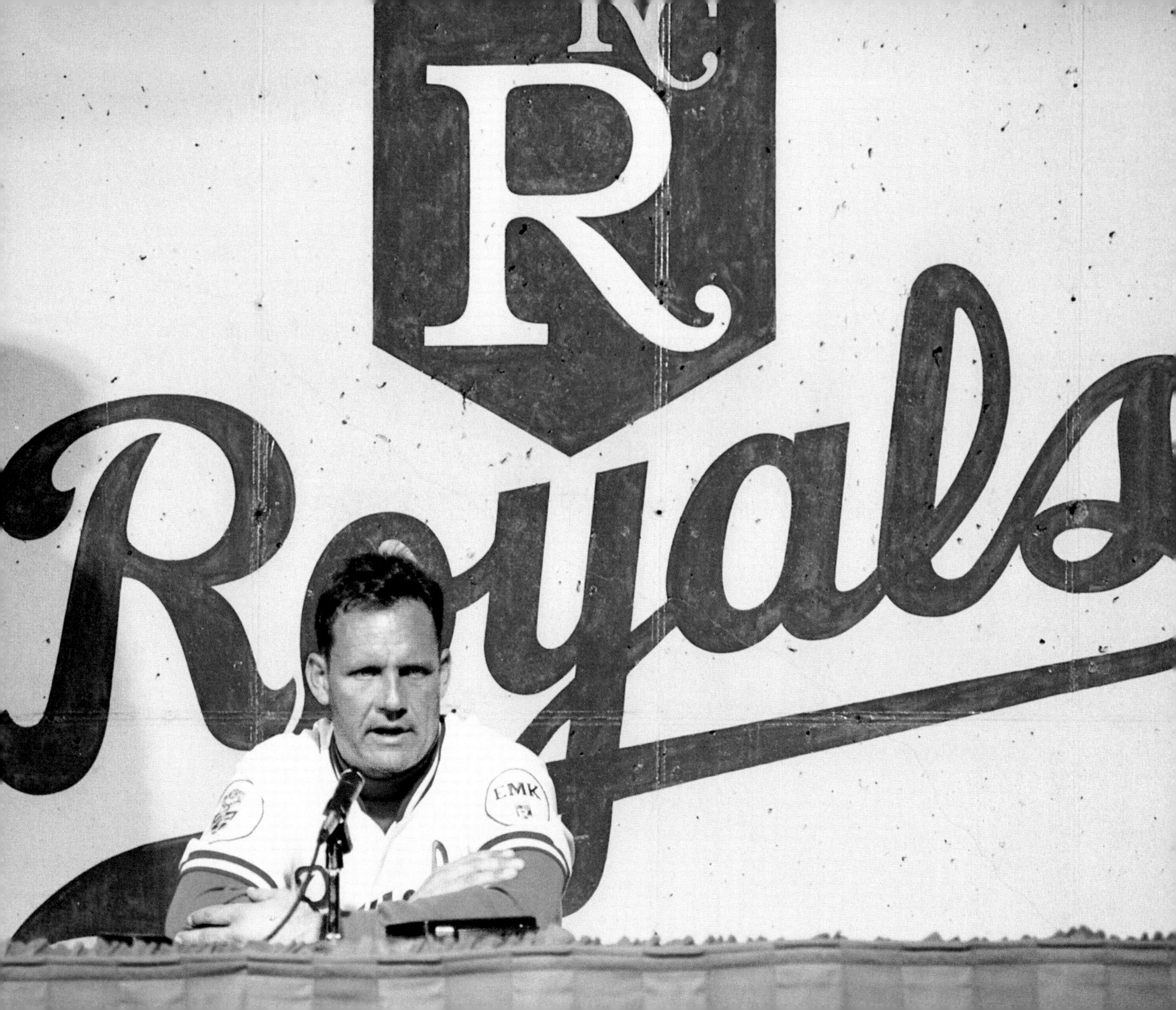
KC
R
Royals
EMK

DEDICATION

To my parents, **Jack and Ethel.** Thanks for the endless hours of **support and love.** You taught me the qualities of life that I will pass along to your grandchildren, **Jackson, Dylan and Robin.**

-George

FOREWORD by Ken Brett

I first met my brother George when he came home from the hospital. My mother said, "Another boy!"

And another boy meant that Jack and Ethel Brett now had a four-man rotation. John was 7, I was 5, Bobby 3 and now George became the latest starter.

One cannot imagine the trials and tribulations the four of us caused while growing up. There was always some sibling rivalry among us. When John got mad at me, I got mad at Bobby. George was the smallest, and he caught it from the three older boys.

I remember one day that we decided it would be cool if one of us could be

ambidextrous. Guess who was chosen? Years later, when I was playing against George in the major leagues, I'd always chuckle watching him actually throwing batting practice left-handed. In the summer of 1966, I graduated from El Segundo High. I was a highly regarded prospect and chosen in the first round of the draft by the Boston Red Sox. I signed 10 days later, but at that time, my father told the Red Sox scout that the real player in our family was the skinny, barefoot 13-year-old - George.

A short time later I caught a break. The Red Sox were going to the World Series and I was going to be eligible. The other two Red Sox lefthanders were out. One had a service commitment, and the other got hurt.

So, at 19, I was going to the World Series. George was 14 at the time, and obviously very excited. Before one game, he actually rode the team bus to the stadium with the players. I'd like to think this was his first glimpse of the future.

We were a very middle-class family. Jack and Ethel loved their children very much. Jack was strict, Ethel loving. Jack had a temper, Ethel was the calm one. When I look back at our childhood, I don't think we lacked for anything.

My brothers and I are all a bit older now, and have never been closer. We would do anything for each other.

It's very easy to love George as a brother. But he has earned my respect and admiration as a player.

All four Brett boys played as professionals, and we dearly love baseball. George was a great player because he respected the game and always gave 100 percent.

Now George has been rewarded with a magical day — induction into the Hall of Fame.
That honor represents a wonderful moment for all the Bretts.

Our Jack passed away too soon for the actual ceremony in Cooperstown, but we know he's smiling from the box seats upstairs.

Jack Brett and his boys (l to r) John, George, Bobby, Ken.

american
little league
of
George BR
el segundo

schedule
1961

El Segundo
Babe Ruth League

EL SEGUNDO RECREATION CENTER

1967

Directory

Gery P Tigers

American

Little League

of

El Segundo

SCHEDULE FOR
1962

STARS
BRILES
MFG COMPANY

MAJOR TIGERS

Manager
Coach

Max Walker
Chuck Brown

NO.	NAME	AGE
3	Bob Green	
4	George Brett	12
5	Bob Fisher	9
6	Paul Burns	10
7	David Hale	11
8	David Walker	10
9	Steve Kastler	11
0	Dick Stump	10
	Jim Helvey	10
	Dennis Jackson	11
	Bob Weber	11
	Russell Fisher	12
	Terry Landreth	12
		12

...ed by:

MARIPOSA MARKET

MINOR TEAM SCHED(ULE)

S - Games played at Stand(ard)
R - Games played at Recre(ation)

	DATE		DAY	HOME TE(AM)
S	April 29		Sun.	Tigers
S				Senators
S				Yankees
R	May	1	Tues.	Indians
R		2	Wed.	Red Sox
R		3	Thurs.	White So.
R		5	Sat.	Indians
R				Red Sox
S		7	Mon.	Tigers
R		8	Tues.	White Sox
R		9	Wed.	Yankees
R		10	Thurs.	Senators
R		12	Sat.	Tigers
S				Senators
S		14	Mon.	Red Sox
R		15	Tues.	White Sox
R		16	Wed.	Indians
R		17	Thurs.	Red Sox
R		19	Sat.	Tigers
S				Red Sox
		21	Mon.	Senators

"George's three older brothers played for me and all were very successful. (Brother Ken was the fourth guy drafted in 1966.) When George was little you could see him playing whiffle ball in the outfield. His brothers said, 'Wait until Louie gets here, he is going to be better than all of us.' (Louie was George's nickname as a little boy.) Guess what-they were right!

When George was a senior I had the entire team take a psychological test. His results recommended that his motivation would improve if I withheld compliments. I did so and George went through the entire year thinking that I disliked him because I never gave him the strokes that others received. Now we look at the test results and have a good laugh.

Also, he could throw with either hand. In our local All-Star Game after his senior year, he pitched to one batter with his right arm and to the next one with his left. He got them both out."

-John Stevenson, baseball coach,
El Segundo High School

C.I.F.
S.S.
19 ✕ 71
Champions

STUDENT COPY
19 71

STUDENT COPY
19 71

STUDENT COPY
19 71

EL SEGUNDO HIGH SCHOOL

STUDENT COPY
19 70-71

NAME BRETT / GEORGE
(LAST)   (FIRST)

Subject Civics   Quarter: 1 ③

Semester: I ⑪

QUARTER   Grade Level: 9 10 11 ⑫

SEMESTER

Achievement: A B ©D F X   Achievement: A B C D F X Larry

Citizenship: E ⑤ U   Kinkoye

Citizenship: E S U

(TEACHER'S SIGNATURE)

The Press Conference

And on **January 5, 1999,** at Kauffman Stadium in Kansas City, with media, friends and family members assembled, the press conference begins.

Good afternoon, everybody. Thanks for coming. I'm Denny Matthews. At 1:00 this afternoon, January the 5th — five, appropriately enough — it was announced that three men had been elected to the Hall of Fame: George Brett, Nolan Ryan and Robin Yount. Brett and Ryan each were named on 98% of the ballots cast. Yount, on 77% of the ballots cast. Obviously, our congratulations go to all three.

George Brett will be inducted into the Baseball Hall of Fame because he connected. He connected for a career batting average of .305, 317 home runs, 1,595 RBIs. He connected for three-one-five-four, 3,154 hits, 1,119 of them for extra bases. He connected for a playoff batting average of .340 and a World Series batting average of .373.

But George connected in other ways. And in even more significant ways. You see, George connected with the game of baseball, its history, its traditions, and he had great respect for how to play the game. George connected with his team, for 20 years, all in the uniform of the Kansas City Royals.

George connected with his teammates, veterans and rookies. He was their leader. He was their example of how to play the game. He was their guy, who would come through in clutch situations.

George connected with his managers and coaches. They all praised how hard he worked, how mentally tough he was and his ability to come through when the going was the toughest.

George connected with the media. You could always count on George for an honest answer, insightful, direct and many times, with a touch of humor.

George connected with the fans. Both in Kansas City and on the road. All fans recognized his great ability and accomplishments and the zest with which he played the game.

George connected with kids. They loved him. He had the knack of immediately becoming one of them, relating to them on their level.

And George connected with this city. Anytime you put the words baseball and Kansas City together, I'm very confident the next two words will always be George Brett.

So, now the man who connected, is connected. He's connected forever more with the immortals of the game in the Baseball Hall of Fame in Cooperstown.

Now, on behalf of the Kansas City Royals, General Manager Herk Robinson.

Thank you, Denny. And good afternoon, everybody. What a very, very special day in Royals history. George, on behalf of the entire Royals organization, we offer our most sincere congratulations to you on your election into the National Baseball Hall of Fame. In our eyes you have always been a Hall of Famer, both on and off the field. Through your efforts, ability and tenacity the Kansas City Royals were able to accomplish what few other clubs were able to accomplish in the 70s and 80s. You were the player that was always there for your teammates and always the driving force to make the Royals a true championship club. From the first day you put on a uniform in Billings, Montana, in 1971, you have been associated with only one team, the Kansas City Royals. This is a feat very rarely accomplished in this day and age. Even today I believe you are the Royals number one fan. You have provided thrills and excitement to millions of fans who have followed and loved you and the way that you played the game. You have won batting titles, been selected as MVP, been inducted into the Royals Hall of Fame and had many other honors bestowed upon you. However, the one that has been announced today will never ever be topped. As of today, you are

George Brett, Hall of Famer and everyone associated with the Kansas City Royals congratulates you and is proud of you. Again, our congratulations to you, Leslie, Jackson, Dylan and a little guy named Robin, whose namesake also had a big day today. George, thank you for everything you've ever ever done for Kansas City.

Now to introduce George Brett, his long-time friend, teammate and confidant, Jamie Quirk.

I'm honored to be here today to introduce to you not only a great baseball player, but also a great friend. (He said don't cry, I'm not gonna, I'm not gonna.) Today George was elected, as the first Kansas City Royal ever into the Hall of Fame. In his 20 years in a Royals uniform, he brought stability not only to the Royals, but also the city. Not to mention a world championship. George *was* the Kansas City Royals. We had some great players, a lot of them are in this room today, but George was our heart and soul. When we needed a hit, he got it. When we needed inspiration, he provided it. George played hard on and off the field. We all know what he has done for ALS over the years. The hundreds of thousands of dollars he has helped raise through his golf tournaments and auctions. As his friend and

teammate for the last 26 years, I've seen many sides of his career, from an 18-year-old shortstop from El Segundo High School to a 40-year-old DH with a knee brace and many more memories in between. Through all those years I've learned some things about George. He personifies the qualities of pride, dedication, sacrifice and, most of all, competitiveness. George hates to lose. Whether it's a friendly golf game on an afternoon, whether it's gin rummy, a bridge game in the clubhouse or a board game at home against Robin, Dylan or Jackson, George wants to win. George never shirked responsibility, he always handled the press as the team spokesman in good days and bad, in a win or loss. He always took the burden as superstars do. There's a quote I repeat to our current players that reminds me of George. "Play the game hard, play the game right, let the numbers take care of themselves." I never once heard George talk about his own accomplishments, he just played the game.

Now it is my honor to introduce the first Kansas City Royal ever elected into the Hall of Fame, **NUMBER 5.**

Well, let me tell you a little story. You don't see any pieces of paper up here because I didn't know until 12:20 this afternoon that I was going to be here. My wife had told me a couple days ago that at 11:00 I was going to get a phone call or I was not going to get a phone call. So, about 15 minutes until 11:00 this morning she said you'd better go to your office and wait for that phone to ring. So I put on a shirt and some sweats and I'm sitting there behind my desk and the phone doesn't ring. I had a few phone calls between 11:00 and 12:00 but not the one I was expecting, or hoping for. Finally, I got the call. Very, very special. Obviously, by my emotions you know how special it is.

I think everybody that ever played the game as a youngster, little leaguer, high school player, minor league player or major league player, has a dream. And that dream is to make it to the Hall of Fame.

I really think it would be a lot fairer for the player if they just gave you the damn election the day after you retire. Because you're used to dealing with the media, you're used to dealing with emotions as a player. I haven't had a lot of emotions going on in my life lately and all of a sudden to get one of the biggest honors in your life is kind of tough to deal with. But there are so many people to thank, where do you start? I guess I have to start with the scout that signed me, Rosey Gilhousen back in 1971. He also signed Jamie. I think he signed everybody on our team ever from the state of California. He passed away a couple years ago, but he's the guy that I believe called up the Kansas City Royals and said, "I have this little shortstop here in El Segundo High School. His brother plays baseball in the major leagues and I think this guy has a chance to be a pretty good player." Tom Ferrick, another one of our scouts, flew out there and Cedric Tallis came out to watch me play. And at the time, in all honesty, I was very, very disappointed when I got drafted by the

Kansas City Royals in 1971. I wanted to be with the Boston Red Sox, I wanted to be a Los Angeles Dodger or I wanted to be a San Francisco Giant, to be honest with you. My brother Bobby said it best. He said, "This is the greatest thing that has ever happened in your career, or in your life, because now all of a sudden you're going to be on an expansion team. And expansion teams, George, aren't that rich in player development in the minor leagues and you might have a chance to move up pretty quickly through the ranks." Well, he was right. I made it to the major leagues in two years. And was able to stay here for 20 more. Obviously, I think the guy that really put me over the hump as a player was my good friend, the late Charley Lau. (George looks heavenward) Thanks guy. We had a very special relationship. Thank you. Obviously, the players that I played with, the managers, you all know who you are. I see a lot of ex-players here. Believe me, I wish everybody could have this feeling. I wish everybody in this room could feel as good as I feel right now. It feels so special. I guess that's all I have to say because, like I said, I didn't know if I was going to be here or going to The Peanut and playing gin all day. Or if I was going to be having some BLTs and, who

knows, maybe Miles (Prentice) would have come in. I took Miles there for lunch one time and I think he's been back every time he's been in town. I guess it's questions and answers for a while, and I'll be happy to stay up here for as long as anybody wants me to answer questions.

No questions? Where's the beer?

Why do you think you got 98% of the vote?

Do you think it was those Christmas cards my wife sent out to all the voters? I think that might have had something to do with it, I don't know. Usually we send about 300 of them out and she sent me to the post office to get 800 stamps. So I don't know what that was about. It worked, hon, good job.

Tell us about getting the call from the Hall of Fame.

Well, Jack O'Connell called and said, "George," and I said, "Yes sir," and he said, "This is Jack from the Baseball Writers Association and I just want to let you know that you've been elected into the Hall of Fame." And I said, "That's very nice news, thank you very much." Then he said, "We had our largest turnout ever of votes. You got 98%." That's when I lost it. He also told me Nolan got 98% and he got three more votes than I did. I thought Nolan was a lock. And then when he told me Robin Yount made it then I lost it again. Of all the people that I've played baseball against in my 20 years, I've never enjoyed playing against anybody as much as Robin. So I was very happy for him.

How do you want to be remembered?

I think as someone who respected the game. Someone who enjoyed it. I mean, I could have played one more year, but if I had, it would have been just for the money. And I don't think baseball deserves that. I knew my skills were declining, I knew the Royals had a guy in Triple-A that they would rather have named Bob Hamelin, who was a great choice. He was Rookie of the Year. I just figured since I wasn't enjoying the game that much, it was time to bid it farewell. That's why I left. I still could have played, I think the year I retired I still led the team in home runs and RBIs, but I just didn't get that enjoyment out of it anymore. The wins didn't feel that great, the losses didn't hurt as bad. A strikeout didn't upset me as much and the success didn't put goosebumps on my arms anymore. The drive to be the best just wasn't there like it once was. It was like going through the motions, and I really believe the game deserves a lot more than that from its players.

What was your greatest thrill?

Obviously, the World Series, winning the World Series. My last home game was pretty exciting. There's so many fun, exciting things that have happened in my career but winning the World Series is obviously the greatest one. I think another big one for me was in 1990. When I had a great second half after hitting .255 in the first half and came back and won the batting title. It was the first time in my career that people starting counting me out, saying I was over the hill and that I should retire. And then to come back and hit over .400 the second half of the season at age 37 and beat Rickey Henderson in the batting race.

I told Avron Folgelman that if it wasn't for him giving me a pep talk in 1984 that this (making the Hall of Fame) probably wouldn't have happened either. He told me, "George, you're making more money on this team than any damn player we got, and you spend half the year on the DL because you don't take care of yourself." He said, "Damn it, I want you to come to spring training next year in the best shape of your life." I hired a trainer and I worked my butt off and I had the best year of my life in 1985. I think if he wouldn't have told me that, that my career probably would have been over a lot sooner, because I would have continued to live the life that I was living up until then. You can do that stuff when you're 20 years old or 22 or 23 or 25, but when you get in your early to mid-thirties, you can't continue to do those things, your body won't recuperate and bounce back day after day. I told Avron that was the greatest inspiration that anybody gave me. I really believe that's why I played 20 years, because in 1984 I got a wake-up call.

Ewing Kauffman and I, we were kind of like father and son. Kind of like my boys with me, you know they love you one minute and hate you the next. Obviously, I had a lot of respect for the man, he did a lot for the Royals organization. We had our disagreements. Unfortunately sometimes they got laundered in the newspaper, which I regret and I think he did too. But I know when he died he knew that I loved him. Hopefully, someday I'll run into him again. His wife Muriel, what a very, very special lady. Mr. Kauffman never really liked, I don't think, to get close to the players. He kind of sat up in his box and watched and gave Joe Burke, Herk Robinson or John

Schuerholz the checks and said, "Go do the best you can, boys." Regardless, he never really did things with the players. I was fortunate to do some things with Ewing Kauffman. In Palm Springs we played golf, he invited me to his house for dinner and things like that. But, during the season, there was nothing like that. I remember one time telling Mr. Kauffman, "You know, Mr. Fogelman has this big party in Memphis for us when we leave spring training." Then I asked, "Why don't you ever have a party like that at your house for us?" And Mrs. Kauffman said, "You guys would destroy our house." See, she thought we were all these rambunctious little kids, that had never seen million dollar vases before. Well, I have yet to see a million dollar vase.

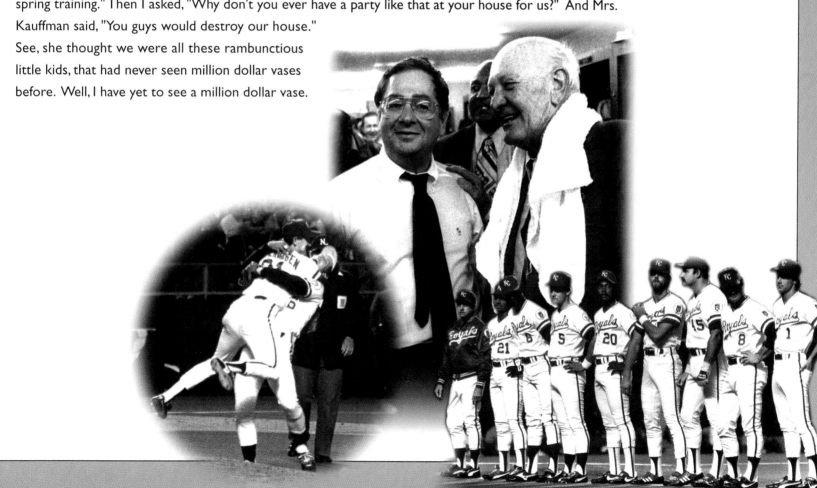

22

1974

1975

1976

1977

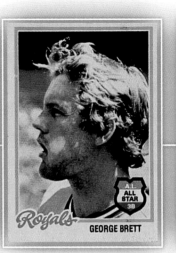

1978

A Hall of Fame Career as a Kansas City Royal:

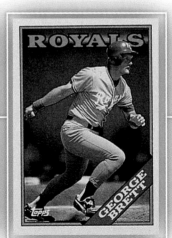

1984   **1985**   **1986**   **1987**   **1988**

1979  1980  1981 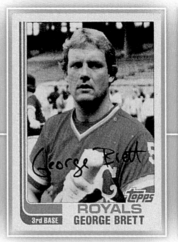 1982  1983

The **George Brett** card collection.

   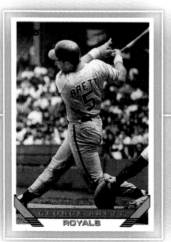 

1989   1990   1991   1992   1993

Reproduced with permission © Topps Company, Inc.

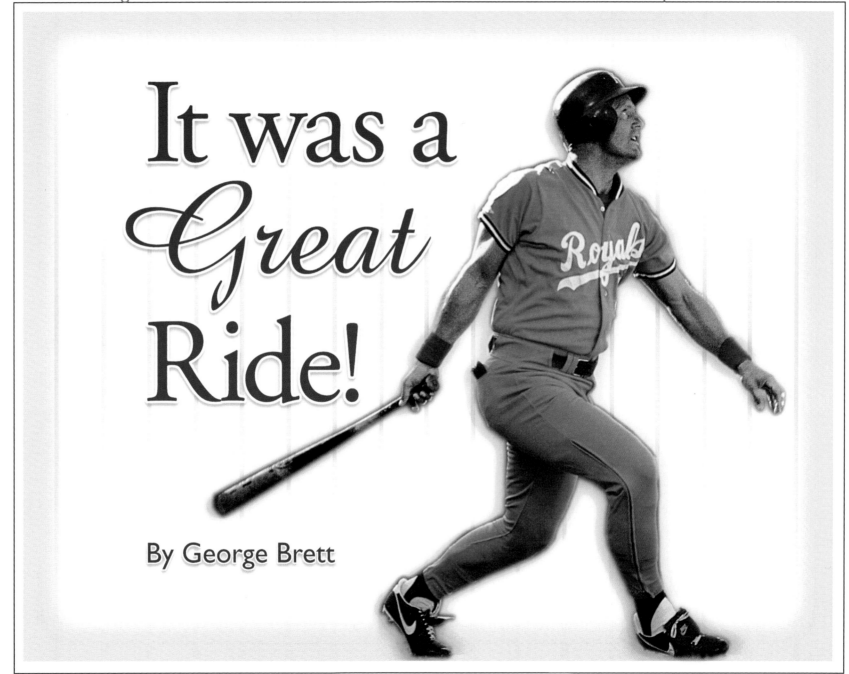

It was a Great Ride!

By George Brett

NATIONAL BASEBALL HALL OF FAME AND MUSEUM, INC.

January 6, 1999

Mr. George Brett

Dear George:

Please accept our heartiest congratulations upon your election to the National Baseball Hall of Fame, baseball's most singular honor.

The upcoming year promises to be a busy and exciting one for you, culminating with your induction on July 25th. We know that you will have a lot of questions about Hall of Fame Weekend and all of the events surrounding your Induction. Rest assured that we will work closely with you in the coming months to make sure that you have all of the information you need to make your special weekend as enjoyable as possible. To that end, since 1994 each of our electees has come to Cooperstown in the early Spring for an orientation session, to get answers to specific questions, and also to learn more about our institution. We believe that each of them has found this visit to be helpful and therefore we would like to extend this tradition by inviting you and your wife to Cooperstown as our guests this Spring.

Each year we ask our electees to sign our standard Enshrinee Agreement, two copies of which are enclosed. In brief, the purpose of this agreement is to grant permission to the institution to use your name and likeness as a member of the Hall of Fame for the production of a plaque to be exhibited in the Hall of Fame; the generation of publicity; and the development of merchandise for exclusive Hall of Fame programs on items such as our Yearbook, plaque postcards, bats and other types of items. As a not-for-profit, educational institution, the Hall of Fame relies upon the revenues generated from the sale of this merchandise to offset operating expenses. In the event you have any questions regarding this document, please do not hesitate to contact us.

For your information you will also find a copy of our 1998 Yearbook and a schedule of events from 1998's Hall of Fame Weekend, as well as information on the Village of Cooperstown, host to the ceremonies and related activities honoring your induction. This will give you a general idea as to what will occur this year. We will provide you with specific information on the 1999 Hall of Fame Weekend in the near future. Finally, we have enclosed a copy of our 1998 Induction Catalog to give you an

25 MAIN STREET, P.O. BOX 590, COOPERSTOWN, NEW YORK 13326-0590
(607) 547-7200 FAX (607) 547-2044

January 6, 1999
Page 2

idea of the merchandise we would like to produce under the terms of the Enshrinee Agreement.

Again, our congratulations to you on joining the world's most exclusive and best known fraternity. We are looking forward to the events this summer in Cooperstown.

Sincerely,

Edward W. Stack
Chairman

Maybe people won't believe me when I say this, but I really didn't know I was going to be elected to the Hall of Fame.

I remember how, near the end of my career, everybody doing an interview would say I was a future Hall of Famer. And I'm thinking: Yeah, well, I'll believe it when I see it. There were times when I was playing, still in the middle of my career, and somebody would bring up the Hall of Fame. I would say something like, "Are you crazy?"

See, I knew how hard the game of baseball was for me. I knew how hard the game was in 1980, when I almost hit .400. It was a struggle every day to go out there and try to do something to

help your team win.

I knew what a struggle it was in '85, the year we won the World Series. It was a struggle every day. It didn't come easily. There was work involved.

There were a lot of times when I was playing third base and I'd say, "Don't hit to me. Hit to Freddie Patek."

No kidding, I knew how difficult it was for me. I never went out there knowing I was going to get two or

three hits. Every time I walked out on that field, I was scared to death. I was nervous. I don't know anybody who, if they care, if they really care about their performance and the performance of their team, isn't going to be uncertain.

You're out there, not knowing that you're going to win, and you're playing in front of anywhere from 15,000 to 40,000 at home, or maybe it's Yankee Stadium and the playoffs. I don't think any baseball player is so sure of himself, sure that he's going to get a

I knew how hard the game was in 1980, when I almost hit .400. It was a struggle every day to go out there and try to do something to help your team win.

couple of hits, not make any errors and help his team win.

When there's all that uncertainty, and your future is still clouded so much by what might happen to you, you're nervous. I don't know anybody who wants to go out there and make a fool of himself in front of thousands of people.

I never got over that, because it meant a lot to me, it meant a lot to my dad, it meant a lot to my brothers back home. If I went 0-for-4, I knew my dad would have a terrible, terrible day at the office, or even after he retired, that he'd have an awful day.

If I got a couple of hits and we won and he felt like I contributed to the team's victory, then he had a great day. And it was the same with my brothers John, Ken and Bobby.

I really think that's one reason why I played the way I did, because I had brothers at home who would kick my butt if I didn't play and hustle the way I did. If my brothers saw me hit a ground ball to second base and not run it out, I would get a phone call, minimum.

My older brother, John, might have jumped on a plane and come down and kicked me all over the place. I guess that's one way you get your work ethic.

You have to remember, too, that my dad and my brothers were never satisfied. My dad was a tough general. He was hard to please. All he wanted was results.

If my dad were still alive and I told him that I made it to

You have to remember, too, that my dad and my brothers were never satisfied. My dad was a tough general. He was hard to please. All he wanted was results.

Cooperstown, he would probably ask, "Why couldn't you have gotten five more hits in 1980?"

That would have raised me to .400, and seriously, when I got home that year, one of the first things he said to me was, "You mean to tell me you couldn't get five more hits?"

I remember one time my father happened to be in town and I knew I'd hear a lot from him because I'd had a terrible game. Steve Crawford pitched for us then and he'd gotten shelled in that same game, so we sat around the clubhouse, drinking a couple of beers, and all of a sudden it's 12:30 in the morning.

We had a big game the next day and I decided I wasn't even going to go home. I'd just sleep on the training table.

I called Les and told her I wouldn't be home and to tell my dad that I'd see him the next day. We would all go out for dinner or something.

So my dad wakes up the next morning. He's probably waiting for me to come out of the bedroom when Les finally comes out. Dad wants to know where I am and she says I stayed in the clubhouse because I didn't want to come home.

I had a better game the next day, and when I saw my dad afterwards, he said, "That's the way to go."

Obviously, there were times like that when I didn't want to hear my dad's criticism, but he really did teach us all the right lessons.

It was about learning to live and not being content with your performance. That's just the way we were taught to be. I never

My wife had talked to a man at the Hall of Fame and he told her that if I got elected, they probably were going to call me around 11 o'clock in the morning. So it was about 10 minutes to 11, and she said, "Why don't you go in your office and wait for the call?"

Some of my friends were with me, sitting around,

took anything for granted, so obviously I never took being in the Hall of Fame for granted.

Which brings back the day I got that call.

Hey, things got pretty scary in that room the day I got the call. In all honesty, I didn't know I would make it. I did not know.

waiting for the phone to ring. We're talking and right at 11, the phone rings and my heart starts beating so fast. I pick up the phone and it's a friend of mine, who says, "Have you heard anything yet?"

Then, after awhile, Steve Fink from the Royals office came over and said they told him the call would come closer to noon. But, in the meantime, I'd had two or three calls, and none from the Hall of Fame.

About 10 minutes after 12, they still hadn't called. These guys who were sitting there with me had been having a lot of fun, but then when nothing happened, it just got quiet. For awhile, nothing was said in the room. Nothing. There wasn't a word said until

name."

It was so silly, but honestly, we were having a hard time finding anything to talk about. We were all wondering about that phone call, and the phone wasn't ringing.

I really did think about how this might be the most disappointing day in my life, because of all the excitement and anticipation. I mean,

about 12:20. Even before that, we had started struggling with things to say. My friend John Ray has traveled all over the world about five thousand times, so I said, "John, tell me a place on the globe that you haven't been to yet."

And John looked at the globe in my office, and finally he said, "Well, I haven't been in this country here, but they changed the

everybody had been going crazy.

The day of the announcement was Jan. 5, and I'd been out of town since Dec. 27, visiting my mother in Palm Springs. We took the whole family, a little trip to get the kids out of the cold, let them swim. My brother Ken came down with his kids, so the cousins got to play with each other.

It was relaxing, but we got back on the night of Jan. 2, and the next morning, I picked up the paper about 6:30. I opened up the sports page — I didn't know what had been written all week because I was in California — and there I am on the front of the sports section, and I'm going, "What the heck is this? This is nuts."

But there's a difference between reading your clippings and believing them. And all of a sudden, I'm there in that room on what's supposed to be this big day, and nobody's phoning. And I was thinking about all the buildup, everything that had been written.

And it was all the anticipation. That was weird, because sometimes when I was playing, I'd read the papers when things were going bad. I'd read them, you know, to boost my ego a little bit, help my confidence. I still go down and watch World Series tapes and hitting films and stuff like that, because it makes me feel good that I've accomplished something in my life.

It's funny what goes through your mind. You know, how could forty-some people not vote for Mickey Mantle? What about the people who didn't vote for Joe DiMaggio?

Sometime after noon, I said, "Maybe I should have played another year."

Then I asked Leslie, "How much longer do I have to sit by this phone? Because I'm not going to sit here all day. I'm not going to sit here until 3 o'clock, because maybe no one's going to call."

I started thinking about how I played in a small town, and maybe that made it harder to be voted in. I guess my feelings were kind of like the way I thought when I played.

I never lived on yesterday. If we had a game on Monday, and I got three hits and drove three runs to help win 4-2, I knew I had a part of that win.

But then, when he told me I had been named on 98 percent of the ballots, I just lost it. I sat there and cried like a baby. I mean, all of a sudden, I just went, "Wow!"

But you have to go out there again the next day, so you can never relax. You can't ever be content, so I guess I was feeling like I wasn't content with my career as a whole.

And so, waiting for the phone call that wasn't coming when everybody said it would, I wasn't counting any chickens before they were hatched.

I really wasn't.

Obviously, I did stick around the house, and then finally the call came from Jack O'Connell at the Hall of Fame.

I was very excited, but I tried to be cool and when he congratulated me, I was just saying thanks, right, uh-huh.

But then, when he told me I had been named on 98 percent of the ballots, I just lost it. I sat there and cried like a baby. I mean, all of a sudden, I just went, "Wow!"

Then Jack told me that Robin Yount had made it, too, and I lost it all over again, because Robin is such a good friend. It was all so overwhelming.

I couldn't believe the 98 percent. I was sitting there and I couldn't talk. It was strange. It gave me such a feeling to think that I had been respected by the baseball writers that way. It's funny, but I don't really think I went out of my way to be nice to them. I always tried to be available, because I thought that was one of my jobs as a leader of the ballclub.

There were times, though, that I thought I was probably hard to get along with, because the game meant so much to me. And my performance meant so much. And the team's winning or losing meant so much. And if we lost, I know I didn't want to sit around talking negatives.

My dad told me in 1985 that he was watching Roy Firestone's ESPN show, *Up Close*, and they had a New York writer on there, talking about the American League MVP vote.

I guess Roy Firestone thought I should have been the MVP in

(cont. on p. 34)

Three for the ages.
New York City, Jan. 6, 1999.

Spending the whole day with Robin Yount and Nolan Ryan, all the hoopla, the media running around doing all these interviews. Being one of three guys and the center of attention in the Big Apple. It was fun.

Everybody that I've talked to says it changes your life drastically. Once they tag you as Hall of Famer it changes your life.

I played with a respect for the game. I played with respect for the past and the future of the game.

(cont. from p. 31)

1985, and Don Mattingly won it, even though the Yankees were fifth or sixth, or something.

Anyway, I never saw the show, but my father told me — and he might have been jerking my chain because he always thought I wasn't nice enough to the media — that Firestone said, "I find it weird that Don Mattingly's team is so far down and yet he's the MVP, and George Brett helped lead the Royals to a World Series championship."

And then my dad said Firestone asked the guy who he voted for, and the writer said he voted for Mattingly. When Roy asked him why, the guy said, "I thought he was more accessible to the media." Maybe my dad made it up, because he was trying to get me to be a better person.

But all those thoughts were going through my head with about a thousand others on Jan. 5.

More accessible to the media?

"He runs hard, he plays hard. He's got a swing that might need to be tinkered with. Defensively, he's erratic, but he plays the game the way it's supposed to be played."

Maybe my father was right.

So, when Jack O'Connell told me about the 98 percent vote, it just blew me away.

You know, I really believe that most of those writers didn't vote for me because of my numbers. I think they appreciated the way I played the game, because they see a lot of guys who don't respect baseball enough to play it the right way.

I remember once I asked Art Stewart, the Royals scouting director, if I could see the scouting reports on me from when I was a kid. I wanted to know what the different scouts and managers wrote about me.

Art got the reports for me and everybody had written that I played with a love of the game. They said things like: "He runs hard, he plays hard. He's got a swing that might need to be tinkered with. Defensively, he's erratic, but he plays the game the way it's supposed to be played."

And I really tried to be that way my whole career, which I truly think is why I got all those votes for the Hall of Fame.

Anyway, once I realized I'd made it, I had to call Robin. It was tough to get through to him, but finally I did and he goes, "Mullet Head, how're you doing?"

I said, "Feeling pretty good. How are you feeling?"

And Robin just said, "Pretty good."

What a conversation. I couldn't resist and I said, "Hey, what are a couple of guys like you and me doing in the Hall of Fame?"

We both got a big laugh out of it, but you know, I think that's the way both of us felt. It almost didn't seem real, even then.

I guess it started to sink in later that day, at the press conference at Kauffman Stadium — seeing so many people I knew, so many friends and ex-teammates that it was incredible — and finally, when we flew to New York.

Can you believe the Hall of Fame people actually gave us fake names when we checked into the hotel? I told them I didn't need one, that I'd never used an alias the whole time I played, but they said that's the way things were done.

The guy said, "You've got to have one, because we've already picked out a name: Pie Traynor (another Hall of Fame third baseman)."

So that was my name.

"Mullet Head, how're you doing?"

I was registered as Pie Traynor, which was pretty funny at the front desk. They were paying for the room, but I was supposed to pick up the incidental charges, so I had to give them my credit card.

Here my room is under the name of Pie Traynor, and I give them a card that says George Brett. The woman at the desk was saying, "I don't understand. These don't match."

And she had no clue who Pie Traynor was. She asked me to spell it, and I wasn't really sure, either. That whole thing was a lot of fun, but somewhere in there, it started to hit me.

The Hall of Fame.

Geez.

My friends and other players and people I know have never treated me any differently than anyone else, I don't think. So it's going to be interesting if I'm, say, with the ballclub and we're playing the Cleveland Indians. I wonder if the players will look at me differently. Everyone tells me that those three words — Hall of Famer — all of a sudden change your life. I'm curious to find out.

One thing I honestly didn't realize was the impact this would have on Kansas City.

My wife had been on a steering committee, in case I got elected.

(cont. on p. 38)

George on Charley Lau

I think a lot of it was repetition, understanding the importance of what good fundamentals were. Rather than just seeing the ball, hitting the ball. Now, all of a sudden, I knew where my hands had to be. I knew where my weight had to be. I knew the importance of swinging through the ball, rather than to it and around it. I knew the importance of being able to hit a line drive to left field or a ground ball between third and short as a left-handed hitter. I knew the importance of all the fundamentals that Charley Lau taught me. And we worked on those things. Obviously, when you feel comfortable with that, it's gonna give you that confidence.

I'll never forget the day I got two hits off Dave McNally. He was a tough lefthander. Two of them were line drives right by his hand. All of a sudden I go, "I got it." Charley says, "You don't have s---. You're not there yet, son, we have a lot of work to do."

We set a goal to hit .250 by the end of the year and within a month I was at .250. I'm going, "I reached it and he says, "No, our goal is .260." I said, "You said it was .250." He said, "Yeah, but you're at .250, we've got to set a higher goal for you." I got to .260. My goal became .270. I got to .270 my goal became .280. I got to .280, got to .292 with four games to go in the season and they fire him. I went 0 for 12 the rest of the year and ended up getting .282. I really think if they hadn't fired him I would have had a chance at .300. He was a security blanket to me. He was there. He was the guy I would talk to after at-bats, he was the guy I'd sit in the locker room with and have a beer. We'd sit there, go over each at-bat, pitch location, why I didn't get a hit, what I did wrong. I remember coming to the ballpark that last home game on a Sunday. I got into the park and Bruce DalCanton told me Charley got fired. I said, "No, there's no way." And he says, "Yeah, he got fired." I went in the back room and I cried like a baby. I went out to the bullpen and threw a ball against the wall as hard as I could for about 10 minutes. The concentration level wasn't there. I went to Chicago from there and went 0 for 9 in the three games and I ended up 0 for 12. And it cost me the possibility of hitting .300. Because my security blanket was not there. Just like my son Jackson sleeps with a panda bear every night. He won't go to bed without that panda bear. I had a tough time hitting all of a sudden without Charley.

(cont. from p. 35)

They were planning all these events, a giant Hall of Fame celebration with a concert, and a black-tie thing with all kinds of big-name people, even a parade or something like that.

It's amazing to me how important this is to the city. I really didn't realize it at all. It's just mind-boggling. I mean, talking about a statue?

Of me?

I still can't believe something like that.

This is almost like getting a chance to go to your own funeral and hearing everybody say nice things about you.

I guess it's pretty special that I played my whole career in Kansas

But how can it be the same for players who went from city to city — even Nolan Ryan?

City, which is something that's going to happen less and less in baseball in the future. At some point, the city and I kind of formed a bond.

That means an awful lot to me.

Think about what happened to Kirby Puckett, who was going to get his 3,000 hits, all in Minnesota, until he had the problems with his vision. They would be throwing him a party like Kansas City is doing for me.

It's like Cal Ripken in Baltimore, or Tony Gwynn in San Diego.

Their cities appreciate what they've done and they celebrate it.

But how can it be the same for players who went from city to city — even Nolan Ryan? Is New York going to do something for

him, or Anaheim, or Houston, or Dallas?

Yeah, they will, but it's not the same thing.

As great as Nolan was, he and some other famous players are

not going to have that close-knit relationship with a city like I was able to have for more than 20 years in Kansas City. Robin played that long in Milwaukee, but he always lived in Phoenix. Is Phoenix excited for Robin? I'm sure his close friends are, but what about the city of Milwaukee?

I realize how much baseball is changing, which is why players now are moving around so much.

It's something to worry about, because there's so much disparity between small markets and big markets. Something's got to be done.

What?

I don't know.

Revenue sharing sounds easy, but if you're George Steinbrenner or you're Disney or you're Ted Turner, do you want to share revenue?

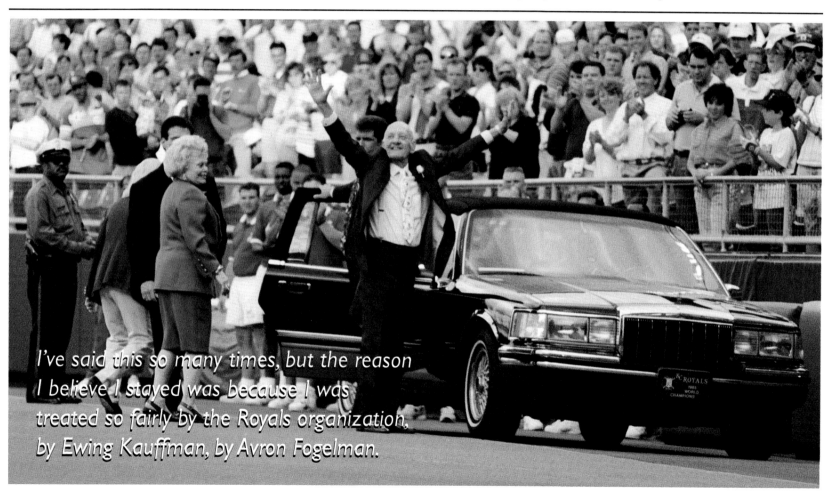

I've said this so many times, but the reason I believe I stayed was because I was treated so fairly by the Royals organization, by Ewing Kauffman, by Avron Fogelman.

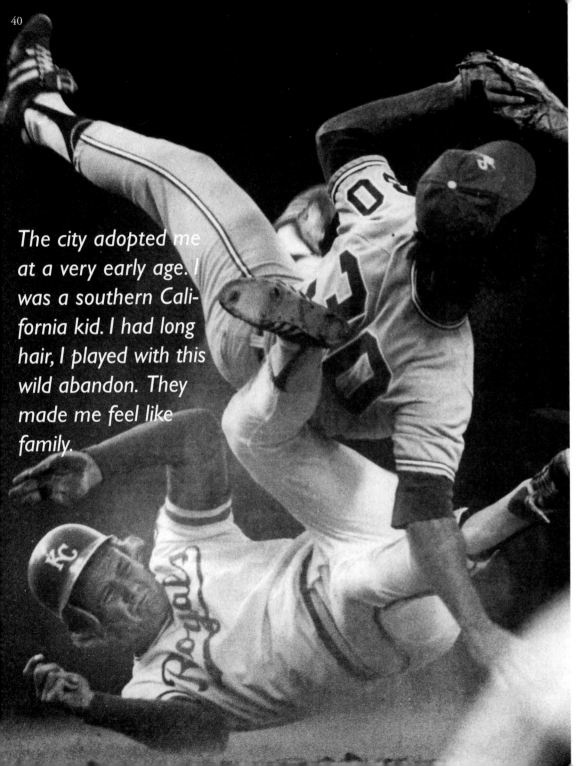

The city adopted me at a very early age. I was a southern California kid. I had long hair, I played with this wild abandon. They made me feel like family.

I do know that when the next big contract negotiations come up, things have to change. John Ray has negotiated a lot of big deals for his company and I remember that he once told me, "George, in any negotiation, if both sides walk away from the signed deal feeling that they've won, then you've got a great deal. But if one side feels it's won and the other side feels it's lost, that deal isn't going to work." I think in most of baseball's recent negotiations, there's been a winner and a loser. Hopefully, this next time we can work out something that both sides — owners and players — feel good about.

It's got to happen, because I really believe that if there's one more work stoppage, you can roll this game up and throw it away. The fans are sick and tired of it, particularly after the NBA thing.

Looking at some of these problems now makes me realize how fortunate I was during my own career.

The more I think back on it, the more I feel like I played at just the right time. The city and the organization were right for me and so I never had to leave.

One thing that made me closer to Kansas City is that for most of the time I played, I was single and I was always out. Before I got married, I think I only went straight home from the ballpark once. I know a lot of people because I met a lot of people. I think I have a closer tie to the city because of that.

Instead of just playing in Kansas City, it became my home, and that's different.

I've said this so many times, but the reason I believe I stayed was because I was treated so fairly by the Royals organization, by Ewing Kauffman, by Avron Fogelman.

The city adopted me at a very early age. I was a southern California kid. I had long hair, I played with this wild abandon. They made me feel like family.

Every time I went to the ballpark, even though I grew up 1,600 miles away and my family all lived on the beach in southern California, after awhile I became a Kansas City guy. Some people wondered why I didn't leave and become a Dodger and move to

I have a wonderful wife and family, with three great boys.

Manhattan Beach. Or why I didn't go play with the Angels and live in Newport Beach. They just didn't understand the relationship that I had with this city.

It was a little bit rocky once or twice, but 99 percent of the time it's been great. Just great. Honestly, that bond I have with Kansas City is just another wonderful thing that's happened to me. It's like most of my life has been one long dream, only it all came true.

I was lucky just to play as long as I did. My brother Ken told me one time that it was amazing, with all the injuries I had — broken shoulders and rotator cuff and the knee problems — that I could even keep on playing. He always said I was so close to getting that big one, the one that knocks you over the head and you know you can't do it anymore.

After my third knee surgery, one of the first things the doctors asked me was whether I ever skied.

I said, "I never have."

They said, "And you never will."

My wife wants to go skiing with the kids, and she asked if I could put a brace on my knee or something. I told her, "Nope, I'll just hang out and you guys can ski." So that's what we'll do for our winter ski outing.

George and son Jackson circa 1996

(cont. on p. 44)

Leslie Davenport

and

George Brett

would like you to join them

at a reception

to celebrate their marriage

Saturday, the twenty-second of February

at half after seven in the evening

Hallbrook Country Club

11300 Overbrook Road

Leawood, Kansas

Royals hitting star George Brett, long the city's symbol of bachelorhood, apparently will wed Leslie Davenport of Kansas City on Feb. 15.

Other details of the impending marriage were unavailable.

This much is known: Brett, 38, has been dating Davenport, 27, for about two years. They met while she was working at a Kansas City store that he frequents. She attended the University of Kansas.

As late as Tuesday, Brett was saying he wasn't engaged. But Thursday word came from the Royals that Brett and Davenport are to be married.

-The Kansas City Star, *January 24, 1992*

(cont. from p. 41)

The point is that I was so lucky, with my health and everything.

I have a wonderful wife and family, with three great boys. I mean, the day I got the call from the Hall of Fame was my son Robin's third birthday. And Jackson's old enough now (6) that he sort of understands what I did for a living.

When we were all sitting around waiting for that call from the Hall of Fame, and I was sweating it out, Jackson came by on his way to school and he said, "Dad, did you get your important phone call yet?"

That's a line I'll never forget.

I keep thinking that I've gotten every break. Honestly, I didn't even want to be a baseball player. I wanted to play in the NFL. But when you're the quarterback of your high school team and then, three games into the season, your coach comes up and says he's

going to make a change at quarterback...well, you realize you're probably not going to make it in pro football.

To play baseball and end up having the career I did, you've got to pinch yourself once in awhile and say, Is that really me, or who's the imposter in my body?

Think about all the people I met, just at the right time, to help all this happen. My high school coach, John Stevenson, taught us to play hard and everyone in my family reinforced that.

I had great coaches after I signed in '71 and went off to play in

— and then there was Hal McRae, who taught me how the game was played,

Billings, Montana. I made it to the big leagues quicker than I ever imagined — even though I never even hit .300 in the minor leagues — and then there was Hal McRae, who taught me how the game was played, and Charley Lau, who really is responsible for everything that happened.

My emotions kind of got away from me a few times at the press conference after the Hall of Fame announcement. But I really did have trouble not just crying and crying when I tried to say thanks to Charley.

The things that have been written and said about Charley, and how he changed my swing and made me a better hitter are true, but Charley was more than that to me. He cared so much. It was a very special relationship.

Charley.

The first time I came up to the big leagues, in 1973, I hit .125. Granted, I didn't get a lot of at-bats and I wasn't in the lineup every day, but I still didn't hit much.

At the All-Star break in '74, we were flying home from Cleveland and Charley put his arm around me on the plane. He wanted to sit next to me.

And then he said, "I think you've got a chance. But you're going to have to change some things. You'll have to be willing to put forth 100 percent effort and trust me, and it's going to be a long, long process. I think you can be successful in this league, but you're going to have to change."

I told Charley then that I had no place to go but up. I was hitting .200 with over 200 at-bats and no home runs and maybe 10 RBIs. So let's do it.

Why not?

"I think you've got a chance."

I gave him the effort he wanted. At 4 o'clock every day at home and 3 o'clock on the road, I had to be at the ballpark for extra hitting. No matter what. And he wasn't kidding about the commitment I had to give him.

One day I didn't show up because I got a little content. That's when Charley gave me the name "Mullet Head." He wanted to know where I'd been and I told him I had a headache. He said, "I don't care if you've got a headache. I said every day. Now you'd better be here tomorrow at 4."

After that, I never missed a day, regardless if I was swinging the bat great or if I was swinging poorly. I don't even like to imagine what would have happened if I hadn't listened to Charley and believed in him. But that was just one more way I was lucky.

You know, when I think of my family, my coaches, the scouts who believed in me, then people like Charley and Hal and Whitey Herzog — sometimes I can't believe everyone was there right when I needed them. All of it seems magical to me. Everything's gone my way. Everything. It's crazy.

I've led a blessed life. There's no doubt about it. I have regrets like everybody else, but a lot less than most people, and I truly know how fortunate I am.

Like the song says: Regrets, I have a few, but then again, too few to mention.

And now I'm in the Hall of Fame.

Is that unbelievable, or what?

-no.5

Saturday

Dear Mom and Dad.- here is you
Long awaited letter. Well Now in
in San Jose. The temperature is
about 105°. What a heat wave.
We are Now playing Lodi Orions
That team from tokyo. We
won Last Night 5-3. i went

on our last road trip we everybody
Visacia. at stockton i we
i went 7-15. including
but not cast 4 hit game
homers. one a cheapey b
That was hit well. homer
stockton. a Left
a Lefty

Mom + Dad - Well its been a long tim
No write so since i'm sitting Here it
Waiting for my check to be delivered
I will write and tell you whats going
on. Bobby just called and said he might
come over tonight. He's driving through
Some mon. That sure would be
great. Woody Hahn (our general
manager is due with my $250.00 check to
any moment. Then a short walk to
the bank. As you probably know we
are in 1st place. I just got back from
IDAHO Falls and we won 2 of 3 game
We have a day off today because
theres a circus on The Baseball
Field. Now its $11.00. And its 82°
theres old timers day here in Billings
sidewalk Sales all over The Place. I
went been getting the Hits but

Wednesday
7-21-71

EVERYTHING is great out here
i'm starting to rip the ball. Last
Night I hit another home run,
a three runner. I ended up-3-6-
really 3-5 but in the last innin
Fouled one off my ankle and
was taken out to put some ice
it to stop swelling. This mourni
hort. I might not play
it is swollen pretty bad.
That And i error, which
tough play I played my
game. My first 3 times
as 3-3 with 5 RBI's.
ot taken out, The coun
with the Bases loade
came in + struck
meat, I would h

Mom And Dad- After a 13 hou
through yellowstone our first tw
here in CALDwell, IDAHO were ra
However we worked out yesterday i
rodea We have perhaps the best
The guys on the team are easy t
with. The Last years shortstop
A Lot of the guys say I better
know I'm better. Today (Sunday)
crew is burning the field. Last N
made the rounds to the guys room
werent in. There in hot water- I
Steve stags from cerritos, a good se
and Joe Zdeb pronounced (Zebb) a
Chicago. A good third baseman. Joe
a rock. When we get back to Bill
going to get an apartment. Randy
Are going in halves and maybe
from Mayfair high might go in.
is really a dead town. I got my gir
wash my cloths for me. The place we
in Caldwell is really Nice. I got a k
bed, color t.V, & air condition. I'm in
method of writing Bobby, Kemer
Say Hi to mr. Norris, & O.B. ok.
here from you soon,

Love Geor

Keeping in touch...

KANSAS CITY ROYALS BASEBALL CLUB
KC R
P.O. BOX 1969
KANSAS CITY
MISSOURI 64141
(816) 241-4101

...M + DAD- Well Now its Thursday at about
I... Just got home from the game.
finally won-- 46-2. Now our record is 1-3.
...aving been doing pretty go...
...once in the four games. I
...t 3rd The Last two games...
...rors, my fielding has impro...
...ed The Red Sox twice and lo...
...6-2. If theres anybody I'd...
...m. Jim Wolford our second base...
...d. Them talking about me...
...n and stuff.) I've been hittin...
...ept for today. So far I'm...
...ary Blaylock said Don't wo...
...ing. I can honestly say...
...ow I could Play Double...
...RIPle A. Lloyd Lightfoot ou...
...layed AA This year and...
...s good as him. Charly D...
...Is No good, He Played AAA.
...Do is Show Them I can...
...Think I will be There.
...isn't That good any more
...get home till about 4:30...

HOTEL FORT DES MOINES
10TH AND WALNUT · DES MOINES, IOWA 50309
(515) 243-1161

Dear Mom + Dad- i am starting to g...
back to the swing of writing again
Now as you see we're in Des Moinse. its
a pretty... good town. Last nite we won
...300. i did pretty good althoug...
...5. i hit the ball good. before
i was interviewed and they
hitting a strong 301. i'm
...about it because i know
...d so do the pitchers on
...eam. in The paper it said
...and 6 RBI's. That dont bother
...i'd send it to you. i want
...bad. i am seeing these
...n The paper that started
...ague Now in The big leagues.
...oing. Good Luck on The house
Love- George

ANOTHER FRIENDLY ... HOTEL
OVER

Holiday Inn OF OKLAHOMA CITY-WEST
P.O. BOX 82625 · INTERSTATE 40 AT MERIDIAN
OKLAHOMA CITY, OKLAHOMA 73108

5-5-73

Folks.

Just a short Note to say hello.
as you see we're in Oklahoma City +
we stay way out of town. We have a
lot of time with nothing to do. So i
thought i would mail you these two
clippings. They don't say much but the
box square does. i've been hitting the
crap out of the ball. my average might
show. about 370-380. its gonna stay
there, too. i went 2-2 off wade Blassigame
and then they took him out. Rats. all
The guys on the team just keep saying
keep doing what you've been doing and
don't get cocky and you'll

Quotes and Memories

"One look at George Brett and you knew

he was a ballplayer.

An authentic ballplayer who would fit and excel

in any era.

He'll be in Cooperstown with Nolan

Ryan, Robin Yount and other great contemporaries,

but The Big Train, The Georgia Peach and The

Bambino would welcome him too. They knew a

ballplayer when they saw one."

-Bob Costas, NBC Sports

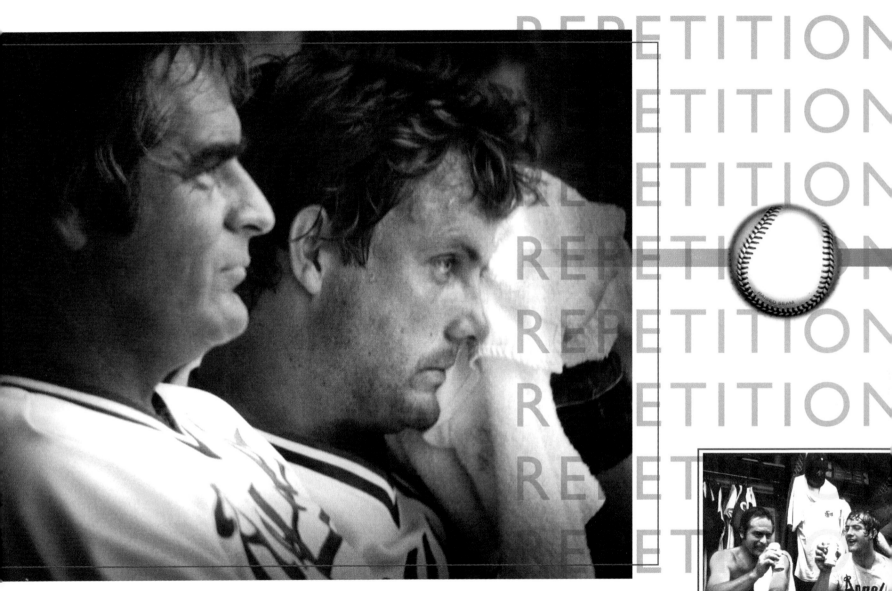

REPETITION
REPETITION
ETITION
ETITION
ETITION
REPETITION
REPETITION
REPETITION
REPET
REPET

"I love George Brett.

see the ball

hit the ball

You're get'n it kid.

George is everything that's right about baseball, and not just because he's a good hitter.

I want you to know that George Brett will never be a selfish player. My only worry about him is that he plays without fear, and that he might hurt himself — end his career. He doesn't fear the baseball, which frightens you.

An injury could cost him. How much? You'll laugh, but if George doesn't hurt himself seriously, someday you'll see him in the Hall of Fame.

I played with Hank Aaron and Eddie Mathews and some other great players. George will be in that class."

- *Charley Lau (1977)*

"George had an aura about him. Right from the beginning, there was something that made him different and exciting."

-John Schuerholz, former Royals executive

53

"The first time I saw him, I knew that he was going to hit. He had that **natural swing** and went on to prove that he could hit."

-Rod Carew, Anaheim Angels hitting instructor and Hall of Famer, 1991

Photo: Visit to the White House after 1985 World Series victory.

"Cooperstown. The ultimate, is a place where George Brett has long been destined to go. He deserves the honor not just because of his tremendous ability on the field, but because of his actions off the field as well."

-President George Bush

"At the time of the 1980 playoffs with the Yankees, I was driving an old junk car, a '64 Chevy. During the playoffs, **George,** as always, sat next to me in the dugout. When he sat down after hitting the three-run homer off Goose Gossage to clinch the Royals' first **American League** title, he turned to me and said, 'There, Al. Now you can get rid of that piece of junk and buy yourself a decent car.' "

-Al Zych, Royals equipment manager, 1969-1988

"In my 57 years in the game, I never met anyone like **George Brett.** I have always thought that he is not only the best ballplayer but the best person I have known. In this materialistic world, he has never lost the common touch. He has always made time for everyone, especially kids. One time, one of the groundskeepers was going to take his date to the prom in his old jalopy and George loaned him one of his best cars to take instead. George was a player that gave **100%** and then some."

-*George P. Toma, groundskeeper*

"Considering what was asked of him, George was great. He signed a million autographs. He signed for every charity deal. Look around at some of the other players today who resent being asked to do anything, and you realize it was amazing how cooperative George was for so long."

-Dean Vogelaar, former Royals executive

"It was the early 70s and from the first day **George** wandered into the Royals p.r. office, so young, with his blond, tousled, curly hair, bright blue eyes, worn looking jeans, and boyish grin, it was love. He plopped himself next to my desk looking completely lost and there was just an instant, special, maternal feeling. His mother called me from California and said, 'Take care of George, he's my baby and he's so young.' I did take care of him for **23 years.** It was as if I had inherited a son.

In the beginning, I never thought he would be famous, but I always knew he was special, with an inner strength and determination like none I had ever seen. He always went the extra mile, working just a little harder to perfect his swing or his fielding.

Watching him achieve greatness through the years has filled my husband Bill and me with a great sense of pride and accomplishment.

We have loved being along for the ride, not only watching his marvelous career, but also being privileged to be part of his personal life. His marriage to beautiful Leslie, the births of Jackson, Dylan and Robin, and making me **Jackson's godmother** are among the most special memories.

It has been a joy to have worked with George and to have been his good friends and confidants. Most of all, we are proud of the good person he turned out to be, and his unending loyalty. We thank him for all of the memories and for sharing his life and family with us."

-Joanie Frey, personal assistant and surrogate mom for 23 years

"**George Brett** is a man for all seasons. Summer-time was prime-time for him. He made it Brett-time."

-*LeRoy Neiman, artist*

"One of my favorite memories of George took place off the playing field.

It was the first year that I was invited to join the Royals team, which, after each baseball season, took a bus trip to Wichita to visit Rainbows United, a school for severely handicapped children.

The way that George interacted with those **kids** was truly special to witness. To them he was just an ordinary guy who became their **hero for the day**."

-John Boyd Martin, sports artist

"One of the most endearing qualities of **George Brett** is his personality and care-free attitude. In my experiences, Lou Holtz and George have been the most cavalier of my sports art subjects. In fact, I had thought that George had a devil-may-care attitude about everything, but there was one exception.

Whenever the subject of baseball entered our conversation, his demeanor and the look in his eyes changed. You can call it intensity, focus or dedication. Whatever it was, you just knew that he was dead serious about the game he loves.

There's no fooling around with baseball with GB!

In addition to his noteworthy skill and career statistics, the Baseball Hall of Fame honor for Brett serves as a lasting tribute to his undying spirit of competition, deserving both our respect and admiration.

It was following his stellar 1980 season that I prepared a graphic arts montage to commemorate **George's** quest of **.400.** This is the display painting owned by Brett that was the basis for a limited edition art print series, which, of course, numbered **390.**"

-Ted Watts, sports artist

"I always had a key to the training room, and I can't remember how many times George would ask to the borrow the key. I knew exactly what he was doing. He'd be hurt one night and you just figured he'd miss a few days.

Then the next morning, he'd let himself in, give himself treatment for whatever it was and, come game time, he'd be in there.

He never made a big deal out of it or acted like a hero, either. He was just a ballplayer who wanted to be on the field, like guys in the old days.

But George was a star, and nobody would have said a thing if he'd rested when he was hurting a little bit. He didn't care. He worked at getting back in the lineup like a guy who was just trying to stay in the big leagues.

I'd see him going home some nights, all beat up, and figure there was no way to get him in there the next day. Then, sure enough, somehow he'd be ready to go and get three or four hits.

That's one part of George's makeup that people outside the clubhouse probably don't appreciate like they could. But it's no accident that other players, managers and coaches respected him so much.

They knew."

-Whitey Herzog, former manager

"...**Brett** steps in, Gossage ready, the pitch, swing and a high fly ball, deep right field, there she goes, HOME RUN, HOME RUN by Brett and the Royals lead 4-2. George Brett hit it in the upper deck off Gossage and the **Royals lead.**"

-Fred White's radio call, Oct. 10, 1980

65

"I'm sure a million people will tell you now that they called it, but this is the truth: I'd watched

George from the time he came up to the big leagues, and he could do anything in 1980.

I was positive he was going to hit a ball deep, and I told myself to be sure before I said anything on the air.

I never doubted he'd hit a ball far enough, really, but I kept reminding myself to be sure it stayed fair. That's a

true story.

I didn't have to worry about it being fair or foul, after all.

The ball got out so fast that it didn't have time to hook an inch off line. It was like Goose threw it

and George just handed it to some fan in the third deck, all in about half a second."

-Fred White, broadcaster (on Brett's home run off George Gossage in the 1980 playoffs)

"I don't know how hard I threw it. I just know the ball went out a lot faster than it

went in."

-Goose Gossage (on the 1980 homer)

JULY 24,

The pine tar bat is on display at the National Baseball Hall of Fame.

1983

People ask me what I was thinking in the Pine Tar Game -

I never had any intentions of hitting anybody. I had just

got out of my mouth, that if they call me out I'm gonna

go out there and kill one of those guys. Well, Tim

McLelland is 6'6" and weighs 250 pounds and he's the

guy with the bat in his hand. I ran out there, and I

started jumping around when Joe Brinkman came up

from behind and grabbed me around the neck and

that's when I was trying to get away, I didn't know

who had a hold of me. It looked a lot uglier

than it was.

-George Brett

"Put yourself in my shoes. Here I was, a rookie umpire, working in the most revered ballpark in baseball, **Yankee Stadium.**

The best reliever in baseball was throwing to a future Hall of Famer. Although a bit nervous, I still had a job to do: calling the balls and strikes in a classic duel—**Goose Gossage** vs. **George Brett.**

When George hit the home run, then-Yankee manager Billy Martin was yelling that the bat had too much pine tar. That it went higher than eighteen inches on the bat-more than the rules allowed. Martin was right.

As I turned to the dugout to call George out, I realized that emotions might provoke an argument.

But I did not understand George's mad-dash charge at me from the Royals dugout. After all, I was just enforcing the rules of the game. And I was right!

Little did I know at the time that this would be one of the most controversial and memorable **umpiring decisions in baseball history.** Looking back, it was an event that would forever mark both of our careers."

-Tim McClelland, home plate umpire, the Pine Tar Game, July 24, 1983

"With all that happened afterward, what got lost was the pitch **George** hit. It almost hit him in the ear, and he **tomahawked** the thing over the right-field fence. It was unbelievable that he could hit that ball."

-Goose Gossage (on the infamous pine tar homer)

...more on the Yankees.

"He's the most consistent hitter I've ever seen. I think George will be able to get a hit when he's 60. My fondest memory is his three-run home run to tie a playoff game with the Yankees. George will be remembered first and foremost for delivering in the clutch, many times. I really think that he could get out of bed on New Year's Day and hit a knee-high slider into the fountains at Kauffman Stadium-absolutely."

-Cookie Rojas, former teammate

"It was an **honor** to play with **George** for all those years and I was literally closer than about anyone because I played shortstop.

And I really do feel a special bond with him because I was on base when he connected with the two most memorable hits of his career-the famous **pennant clinching** three-run homer in 1980 and the infamous pine tar home run in 1983. Both were hit off Goose Gossage and both happened in Yankee Stadium.

I have a framed picture of me jumping on home plate just ahead of George in the Pine Tar Game. The Yankee batboy is in the background picking up George's bat. After a few other people fumbled around with it, **Billy Martin** gave it to the umpire, and, well, the rest is history.

I particularly cherish that memory because, thanks to George, I will forever be a part of baseball lore."

-U.L. Washington, former teammate

New York Yankees

GEORGE M. STEINBRENNER III

TAMPA OFFICE
LEGENDS FIELD
1 STEINBRENNER DRIVE
TAMPA, FLORIDA 33614
(813) 281-9001

March 19, 1999

The rivalry between the Yankees and the Kansas City Royals became as good a rivalry as we've had in the twenty-five years I've been in the game. That rivalry was certainly accentuated by the presence of one George Brett. He was a consummate competitor, as much as any man as I've seen in the game. He loved to beat you but he was also gracious in defeat because I believe we beat him a bit more than he beat us.

I will never forget the pine tar incident and how infuriated he was when we called for the bat. The rules were the rules and technically I still believe George was in the wrong. But, Lee MacPhail in his infinite wisdom decided that you had to bend the rules a little. While I underwent suspension because I was so outspoken about it, I kind of had a short smile on the one side of my mouth because it was Brett that had done it to us.

I'm glad he is in the Hall of Fame and I'm glad it was on the first ballot because I don't know too many people that deserve that anymore, if there are any, than George Brett.

Best regards,

George M. Steinbrenner

"In my first encounter with George, I was watching batting practice on the day I purchased half of Mr. K's ownership of the Royals. I had owned the Memphis Chicks AA team for seven years and, to me, batting practice was very mundane. But watching **George's swing** was one of the most beautiful athletic sights I had ever witnessed! It was so fluid, so consistent, so repetitive, regardless of the pitch. You had to see his rhythm in person to believe it. From that day, I knew we could have a world championship club. I had just seen the true definition of a **franchise player,** which I knew was essential to win a championship.

George did not disappoint me. His defensive skills were far better than I had imagined, and he was a really tough third baseman. Smashed teeth, torn knees, he experienced it all playing on carpet as slick as a marble tabletop. At one point in the 1984 season, I could see George's interest began to drift. He was unmarried, ownership was changing, his salary situation was up in the air and he was getting older. He wasn't the same guy I had met just a year earlier.

During the off-season, I visited with George a few times, and suggested that it was time for him to **rededicate** his career to winning the World Championship. He still possessed the greatest swing in baseball, but he just didn't have that same focus. Even at that, George was still an extremely **hard-nosed** ballplayer.

George agreed, and when he sets his sights on a goal, watch out! He got himself into the greatest physical condition imaginable, and the **1985 season speaks for itself!**

All in all, George embodies all the qualities of not only a great baseball player, but more importantly, a wonderful person. He had such concern for other players as evidenced by what he did for Bret Saberhagen, Mark Gubicza, Buddy Black and so many other rookie ballplayers he took under his wing. He knew the importance of them immediately becoming part of the team. The way George accepted each of them was an important element in making our team champions.

He continually impresses me with his intelligent, pragmatic insight in evaluating baseball talent. He is always on target! It seemed only logical that after he retired he would be a truly **outstanding baseball executive,** and he is.

He is a special guy who deserves every honor he receives. He worked hard for it, earned it, with priorities and values that place him as a true American role model. Everyone in America would be a better person if they knew and emulated George Brett."

-Avron Fogelman, Chairman, Fogelman Properties and 50% owner of the Kansas City Royals, 1983-1991

There may not have been one chance in a thousand that he would **beat out** some of those balls, but he **hustled** hard anyway. He never loafed in his life.

And with George, the team always came first. His goal was **winning** for the Royals instead of worrying about his own statistics like so many other selfish players."

-Ewing Kauffman, Royals founder and owner (1992)

Robin, are you 98% sure or 77% sure of that?

© Miller Brewing Co.

"I always loved to **compete** against George. He played the game the way you want to see it played. **He was fun to play against.** **He's fun to be around."**

-Robin Yount, friend and fellow Hall of Famer

"From my short stint at the Royals, it was obvious **George** was the backbone of the organization. He was probably the only person that I allowed to call me **Bobo** and get away with it."

-Bo Jackson, former two sport all-star

"Here's a guy who didn't take his **talent** for granted, who didn't think the world owed him a living. Some of the young players coming along now — if they did half the things George has done — they'd be charging a hundred bucks just to say hello.

But **George hasn't changed** since he was a kid. He loved playing the game, he realizes how lucky he is and he never forgets that."

-Jamie Quirk, friend and former teammate

"I don't think there's ever been a **better hitter** in clutch situations, at least not since I've been around.

I was always a good RBI guy, and I trusted myself to be the guy on the spot. I always said I wouldn't want anybody else up there. **Except George."**

-Hal McRae, former teammate and manager

"It was my pleasure to have **George as a teammate.** He came to play and gave it all he had. He is a real pro, a real player and a real friend. He was the **best clutch hitter** I ever saw."

-Frank White, former teammate

"I remember in 1984, I was just another rookie trying to get settled in Kansas City after making the Royals big league roster. George was **simply the best**. He let me stay at his house, borrow his Bronco(not the Mercedes, though), and generally **'hang out in style.'** He set me up to start looking for my own place, eventually. It was just great having him around during that early, transitional part of a ballplayer's life."

-Bret Saberhagen, former teammate

"I suppose it could be because they are more recent, but my favorite memories of George are those after he was out of baseball. The way he handles himself, always being there as a friend, just being a good person, a good **humanitarian.**

In reminiscing, though, thoughts of George as a player are **unforgettable.** He worked harder than anyone else. His accomplishments as a player fill the record books. I remember thinking, 'How many times can this guy **come through in the clutch?'** He did it so many times. He was like today's Energizer Bunny. He kept going and going, doing and doing. He could handle all cases. And a great guy, a great friend to boot."

-*Fred Patek, former teammate*

"In 1980, during my first year managing the Royals, we were on a road trip, I think down in Texas, early in the season.

I wanted to talk to George about the year ahead and what I thought he should shoot for. I remember telling him that, in my opinion, he was an **MVP-style** player and that he should be thinking of himself in those terms.

His response was that he really was not that kind of ballplayer. He saw himself, yes as a good hitter, but not a power-type, home run hitter. Just a **consistent** contact hitter.

Guess what? George was the **American League MVP in 1980,** batting that incredible **.390** in the process. And home runs? Well, he had 24 during the season, and saved his most memorable round-tripper to clinch the Royals' first American League pennant in the ALCS. That unforgettable, mammoth three-run shot off of Goose Gossage."

-Jim Frey, Royals manager, 1980-81

Office of the Commissioner

MAJOR LEAGUE BASEBALL

ALLAN H. (BUD) SELIG
Commissioner of Baseball

"It has been a privilege to know George Brett and to have witnessed his great Hall of Fame career unfold. I remember well the 1980 season and the spectacular success George had as he flirted with a .400 batting average late into the season. Athletes who experience such extraordinary success often describes themselves as being "in the zone." Well, George was in the zone that year and was well deserving of the American League Most Valuable Player Award.

"The Kansas City Royals and Milwaukee Brewers forged an exciting rivalry during the 1980s, and it was especially gratifying to me to witness the competitive relationship between George and the Brewers' Robin Yount, two of the best players of their era turn into a close friendship.

"George not only was a magnificent baseball player and athlete, but he is an outstanding citizen and human being. He has brought great joy to the game of baseball."

--Allan H. (Bud) Selig
Baseball Commissioner

777 E. Wisconsin Avenue
Suite 2010
Milwaukee, WI 53202
(414) 225-8900 / Fax (414) 225-8910

 "I was in Kansas City for the 1980 World Series when George came down with hemorrhoids. I went up to visit him in his room after he came out of surgery. Of course, my first concern was his **well-being** and that he wasn't in too much pain. Not George. His first words to me were, 'Mom, don't you dare tell anybody about this.'

Five minutes later we heard on the radio, 'George Brett, star third baseman of the Kansas City Royals, just underwent surgery for hemorrhoids.' "

-*Ethel, George's mom*

Brothers Ken, John and Bobby

"Being the first of the **Brett boys,** I did not know what the future held. For a while I thought that I was going to be an only child until my parents added three more boys, to make up the '**Battling Bretts,**' as we were sometimes called.

Since I was the oldest, I was able to hit the most, Ken, or 'Kemer,' pitched, Bobby fielded, and George was always shagging because we never let him hit. John Stevenson became our coach and the 'Rec Park' was our home while growing up in El Segundo, California.

Ever since Kemer, Bobby and I were able to play whiffle ball in our backyard, George would tear at his playpen to get a chance to play like his older brothers. The truth is that his career is the envy of all his brothers. One of my fondest memories of him is when I was playing baseball and I would see him hanging on the fence with his fingers or running around the ballpark, chasing foul balls. Between the hot dogs and the candy, he did not have a care in the world. His nickname during his youth was '**Looney,**' from the cartoon series 'Looney Toons.' It evolved into Lou and Louie.

Today I still see the sparkle that we share watching each other during our baseball careers. I will never forget being at Kauffman Stadium as George's eldest son, Jackson, watched his dad on the field. It makes me wonder how the Brett tradition will continue."

-John Brett

"George was first **invited to major league** spring training camp in 1974. One day while I was taking some ground balls at third base in Fort Myers, this voice behind me said, **'Mr. Schaal, can I take a few ground balls with you?'** Well, I turned around and this long-haired, darkly-tanned California kid was standing there. Even then, George exhibited an air of confidence. I remember my first days in a major league camp. I was tentative, intimidated and afraid to say much. Not George! Well, George was brought up in mid-season in 1974 and I was traded to the California Angels. The rest, as they say, is history. I am now a chiropractor in Overland Park, Kansas, and George was a patient of mine in his playing days. Occasionally, even now, he comes in for treatment when his back acts up. **I now tell my patients that it took a Hall of Famer to take my job from me.**"

-Dr. Paul Schaal, former Royals third baseman

88

"I first met **George in 1976** when I was living in Kansas City. One thing that I've learned about meeting famous or well-achieved people is that you're usually disappointed. However, George was all I could have hoped for and more.

I ended up working in the sales department of the Royals in 1980. George was pursuing his **.400 season** and everybody, worldwide, wanted a piece of him. We tried to shield him from this, as not to distract from his on-field pursuit.

Olathe Night was one of our biggest events at the stadium and to kick off ticket sales for this game, there was a special luncheon with Jim Frey as the big draw. Well, he canceled at the last minute and all I knew to do was lean on George. **Without any hesitation,** he said that as long as Jamie Quirk would go with him he would do it. They both went and it ended up being the best Olathe Night luncheon ever. The crowd was not expecting George and when he showed up, they just went crazy.

George didn't do it for the money or the recognition. He did it to make the team and the organization look good and to help out a friend. He made me look better that day than I could have ever made myself look."

-Rush Limbaugh, friend and radio personality

...some final thoughts and memories.

"It was probably the late 70s and the Royals were playing the Baltimore Orioles in Kansas City. George was 4 for 4, had hit for the cycle (an extremely rare feat, he only did it twice in his career), with his last hit sending the game into extra innings. Then, to top it off, he hits another home run, winning the game and making him 5 for 5.

Orioles manager Earl Weaver went crazy, yelling at his pitcher. Everyone always talks about his playoff and championship games but this is the one that I remember most."

-Ed Molotsky, longtime friend

"It was an amazing thing. Even if you weren't from Kansas City, even if you were never particularly a Royals fan, I think everyone rooted for George Brett."

-Chris Berman, ESPN

"Maybe you get spoiled when you watch somebody so long that eventually you take what they do for granted, no matter how spectacular it is. But as time went on, you realized that George Brett belonged to the history of baseball instead of just to the Royals. This is a once-in-a-lifetime ballplayer."

-Herk Robinson, Royals executive

"I always loved the way he played the game of baseball, and I also thought he was the most dangerous hitter I ever faced — certainly in the American League.

Back with Cincinnati, I used to walk the Giants' Willie McCovey all the time because he could just kill you. I thought I'd never treat another hitter that way, but I wound up doing it with George.

It got to the point where, if the game was on the line, I told our pitchers not to throw a strike. Never. *Roll* the ball up there if you have to."

-Sparky Anderson, Manager

3000

September 30, 1992

"Probably my favorite memory of George is the night he got his 3,000th hit. He was **four hits short** and the doctors had said that he would probably not be able to get the remaining hits **due to a shoulder injury.** I was sitting on the bench as he got his first, second, and third hits. When he got his fourth I just sat there, not believing what I had just seen. **A man who shouldn't have even been playing had just gotten four hits.** After taking a moment to reflect, I joined everyone on the field to celebrate. I will never forget that night as long as I live."

-*Mark Gubicza, former teammate*

"A man by the name Nabil Haddad, the owner of 10 area restaurants, was a supporter of mine for mayor. He held a fund-raiser for me at Figlio. George was there and one of the items up for auction was a painting of a sailboat by Senator Ted Kennedy. George had the highest bid and afterwards came up to me and said, 'Guess what I'm going to do with this painting? I'm going to give it to my good friend Rush Limbaugh.' I'm sure Rush Limbaugh enjoyed receiving a painting done by one of his favorite senators."

-Emanuel Cleaver, mayor Kansas City, Mo., 1991-1999

George with baseball legend Buck O'Neil

"When I met George Brett some 20 years ago, it was right after his rookie season. I was friends with his brother Ken. When George came into town he told me, 'You're a friend of my brother's and in the Brett family when one of us has a friend, we all have a friend. So, sure I'll wear your shoes.' We eventually did a George Brett shoe, the GB5, which was a best seller for two or three years. A good, long-term friendship grew from this working relationship."

-John Fisher, CEO, Saucony Inc.

"The fact that George and Leslie gave their second son, Dylan, the middle name of Richman, because neither my late brother Milton nor I had anyone to carry on our name, probably meant as much to me as anything in life."

-Arthur Richman, senior advisor, New York Yankees

"I was in Milwaukee for a tournament and we went to see the Royals play. Dick Howser had given us box seats right next to the Royals dugout .When we were hanging out in the clubhouse before the game George gave me a Royals shirt to wear. We were sitting in the front row by the batter's box with our feet sticking out from under the railing of the dugout. I was wearing white shoes and as George walked to the box he turned his head and spit some tobacco juice. Of course, it landed smack dab on the middle of my shoe! The tobacco left a stain and I could never wear those shoes again. We always laugh about that."

-Larry Ziegler, Senior PGA golfer

"When I went to see then-owner Ewing Kauffman about renegotiating George's contract, he acknowledged that George meant so much to the community and to the team that he would add $1,000,000 every year to his salary (he called it an 'appreciation bonus') and said that he would put him in his will. I have been an agent for 19 years and have never heard an owner speak so affectionately about a player."

-Dennis Gilbert, former agent

"The term 'Big Leaguer' takes on a whole new meaning with George Brett. He's a big leaguer not only in baseball circles, but also in his commitment to his family and community. This guy is a Hall of Famer to those who aren't even fans of the game. Every major league city dreams of having a George Brett."

-Ted Waitt, Chairman and CEO, Gateway

"George played with the joy of a 13-year-old in his first season of Babe Ruth League. To watch him you'd think this must be his last game...no one could play at that pace forever.

George was able to deliver whatever was needed...down by three in the seventh, a three-run homer...tied in the bottom of the ninth, a grounder stretched into a sliding lead-off double. With a bat in his hand, he was as tough an out as any pitcher ever faced.

From his whisker-stubbled, sun-baked face, to his pine-tar hardened hands, to his knee-high blue socks, George was a ballplayer."

-Buck Martinez, former teammate

"I remember a four-game set with Baltimore in 1984. I was scheduled to pitch the fourth and last game. We had lost the first three games and were playing a Sunday game in old Memorial Stadium to conclude the series. It was a typical July day in Baltimore, scorching hot and so muggy you couldn't see the center fielder from home plate. We had not been playing particularly well and I was scuffing right along with everyone else. My last three or four starts left something to be desired.

Anyway, George came up to me in the clubhouse before the game and says tongue in cheek, 'Blackie, we got'em today.'

I replied, 'Lou, are you sure?'

He said, 'Yeah, no team ever loses the fourth game of a four-game series on the road, especially when it's a Sunday day game.'

That was George's way of making me relax and giving me the confidence not to worry about how I was pitching of late or how the team was playing.

That day George went out and made six or seven fantastic plays behind me at third base, probably the best defensive day I'd ever seen a third baseman have, and we beat the Orioles, 2-1. The confidence I got from George's pre-game talk stayed with me throughout my career. I'll never forget it. We went on to win the A.L. Western Division title that year."

-Buddy Black, former teammate

"George was an outstanding teammate, leader and player. Whatever the situation was during the game, he had a formula for it. What was most amazing was watching him hit .400 for 2 months in 1985 when we won the World Championship."

-Jim Sundberg, 16-year major league veteran, 6-time Gold Glove catcher.

"George Brett was the ultimate competitor; one of the greatest gamers of all time and an outstanding leader. He had the best combination of power and average of his era and was a great clutch hitter. George was one of the few hitters I would take time to watch take batting practice, because of his great swing."

-Lou Piniella, manager, Seattle Mariners

"I don't know anyone who played the game harder than George Brett. His talent and desire carried him on to an illustrious career of 3154 hits, 300 homers and 200 stolen bases. You just can't do any better than that. I've heard he chose to wear number 5 because of me. I'm honored."

-Brooks Robinson, Hall of Famer

"He not only played the game right, he played it extremely well... If I have a son and he loves to play baseball, the best way to teach him how to play will be to show him a video of George Brett."

-Steve Palermo, former American League Umpire

"About 10 years ago, George, Jim O'Bradovich, Daryl Cousins, and I were playing golf at The Vintage, an exclusive club in Palm Springs. George and I were playing against Daryl and Jim and they were playing pretty poorly. On one hole, after their drives went into the desert and our drives were in the center of the fairway, we were on the green in 2. Then both of them made the shots of their lives and were also on in 2. After they made par, George and I both 3-putted. George was so mad that he threw his clubs into the lake and left them there, with his name on them and everything! The three of us played the remaining three holes while George sat in the cart fuming, refusing to talk to anyone."

-Bob Lowe, long-time childhood friend

"The first time I saw George Brett play baseball, it was obvious that he was going to be something special. His swing was fluid and powerful. He had not been with the Royals very long before everybody at the ballpark was looking for his turn at bat. Just watching him swing at the baseball was exciting. His aggressive style of play was equally exciting. George became extremely popular, but he did it the old fashioned way-he earned it.

The thing I admire most about him is his sense of loyalty and responsibility to his friends and fans. On several occasions George has been kind enough to attend a golf tournament we have in Bozeman, Montana, to raise money for athletic scholarships at Montana State University. His willingness and ability to make our sponsors feel comfortable and appreciated is truly exceptional. The folks in Montana appreciate his integrity and down to earth behavior. He has become a favorite in the Big Sky State.

Obviously, George Brett is a gifted athlete and also an outstanding person. But above all, he made it to Cooperstown because he is a tremendous competitor."

-Jan Stenerud, former Kansas City Chiefs kicker

"The first time I met George he was 12 years old and I was giving the Brett family a dog. I knew his brothers from coaching them in basketball. I remember that George had so much enthusiasm and love as he played with their new dog. Over the years I watched him play baseball with that same relentless energy and love of the game.

Now as my real estate partner, George still shows that get-up-and-go in business whenever we purchase new properties.

After all the fame and success he has achieved, George still maintains that same vigorous love of life that I saw in him over thirty years ago. In today's world that is a rare quality."

-Cliff Warren, long-time friend

"Early one spring during a time of stalled negotiations with the Royals, George came to California. He decided to go surfing with the boys from El Segundo, who still surf when they can find the time. George, Jim and Steve O'Bradovich, Steve Bryant, Bob Lowe, Mark Cameron and myself went to 26th Street in Manhattan Beach. It was a slow day, there were not many waves to catch, especially for a novice like George. To pass the time, most of the guys pulled out a little dip from inside their wet suits to help them relax and enjoy the day. This of course sounded good to George and he joined right in. Well, there we were, talking about life and being with nature, all the while spitting tobacco juice in the ocean.

George got restless and decided to paddle south to his brother Bobby's house on 14th Street. So, off he went, dip in mouth, paddling against a northerly drift. Not that he was ever in trouble, but the distance was a bit farther than it looked. This in combination with the dip and the drift caused him to end up on the sand, lying on his board. He was tired and sweating like a dog, his face as green as the waves he had just left."

-Craig Cousins, long-time friend

"George is a great individual. He was just what a young franchise like the Royals needed in the mid-70s. He 'made himself' into a third baseman. He was obviously an exceptional hitter who played the way we did in the old days - giving 100% on the field, every single day. I know that the Royals and Yankees had some heated playoff games in the 70s and in 1980, as well as the famous Pine-Tar game in 1983. Some people might even say that George hated the Yankees. Well, I'm an ex-Yankee. Even so, George and I remain friends-and I am sincerely happy about that."

-Hank Bauer, former Yankee great

"I've known George since kindergarten. Anything he ever did — if it was basketball, he made the big basket; baseball, he got the big hit; fighting, he got in the first punch.

It's happened so many times, nothing amazes us that he does.

With George, it's like: Well, what else did you expect?"

-Steve O'Bradovich, long-time friend

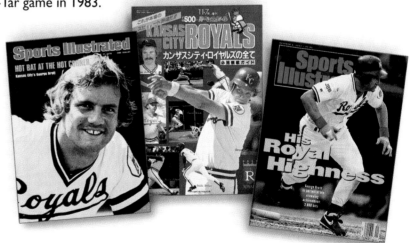

"I don't think there's ever been a better hitter in clutch situations, at least not since I've been around.

"I had the privilege to room with George and then eventually manage him, and I've been there for just about every one of his big milestones.

Something people should know is that from the time I met him, George worked longer and harder to be great than anyone I've seen at that level.

You see reserve players, guys trying to make it into the big leagues, out for early hitting. How often do you see a guy doing it who was already a lock for the Hall of Fame?"

-John Wathan, former teammate and manager

"One of the things I'll remember most about George is that I don't think I've ever seen anyone who really enjoyed playing the game as much as he did."

-Peter Gammons, ESPN

"I've known George a long time and played as his teammate. I've seen him do a lot of spectacular things, winning pennants and everything.

But that day, when you consider the circumstances and all, that was the biggest thrill I've ever had in baseball. Honestly, it was incredible.

I told my son that we might never see anything like it again. I get goosebumps just talking about it."

-Al Fitzmorris, former teammate (on Brett's game-winning, 10th-inning homer the day after he announced his retirement in 1993)

"George is one of those rare people who can walk with paupers and dine with kings. He has never changed. He is not only a great player, but a great person.

He made it easier for me to be accepted among the Royals because teammates tend to follow other teammates and, from day one, he treated me with respect.

I could tell one of the many stories I have about George, but one story would not do him justice."

-Karen Kornacki, KMBC TV-9, Kansas City

"When I think of George Brett, I think of commitment. Commitment to his team, to his fans, to this city, to his long-time fight against ALS (Lou Gehrig's disease) and most of all, his commitment to his family. He could live anywhere and do anything he likes but he's committed to living here and contributing to this community. That's commitment.

That's George Brett."

-Frank Boal, Fox 4 Sports, Kansas City

"I am one of those fortunate reporters that has been around long enough to have covered George Brett from his very first game with the Royals to his very last. All of his great moments on the field will live in the minds of all of us for a lifetime. I especially remember a moment off the field that best describes what Brett is all about.

It was late in his career and very late in the day, long after the morning spring training had ended down in Baseball City. The players had left for the day hours earlier, but as I was leaving, having finished a satellite TV report for KCTV, the crack of the bat was still ringing from one indoor batting cage.

It was Brett, 'Still working on a part of my swing,' he told me. Brett was a great hitter, but like all the great ones, he was willing to pay the price to be great, even in the twilight of his Hall of Fame career when he had nothing left to prove."

-Don Fortune, KMBZ 980 Sportsline, Kansas City

"At least 3 or 4 times while I was sitting next to George on the bench, he would say, "I'm going to go deep" on a certain outfielder. Then, sure enough, he would. To be able to do that is just amazing. Sometimes he would be so hot that you would almost wish that he would have a small injury that would keep him out for a couple of games so that when he came back, he would be on fire again."
  -*Billy Connors, director of player personnel NY Yankees, former pitching coach, KC Royals*

"I only played against him for 3 years but I can say one thing, he was a tremendous ballplayer. Now he is going to be inducted into Cooperstown which shows what everyone thinks of him. I'm very happy for him, he's what the Hall of Fame is all about."
  -*Hank Aaron*

"George Brett has said many times how blessed he feels. But it seems to me that millions of baseball fans probably feel that the reverse is true, as well. How fortunate we've been to watch this once-in-a-lifetime athlete play America's game the way it ought to be played.

It doesn't surprise me a bit that so many fans named their sons Brett.

Why not?

If you wanted a role model, someone you could tell that little boy was his namesake, who better than George Howard Brett, a guy who worked like a demon to succeed and grew into a Hall of Famer?

And became a true man's man, to boot.

If the cheering multitudes felt lucky, I can only say I was privileged beyond imagination to see George from close, close range from the very beginning -- and follow his career every step of the way.

Members of the media are human, too.

We grow to have favorites among the players we cover. No matter how fiercely we seek to be objective, some of these people become special.

Some even become friends.

It's almost impossible for me to imagine any journalistic experience -- anywhere down the road -- which will compare with the thrill of being part of the George Brett Era in Major League Baseball.

This is George's book, so for once, I think I'll keep my nearly endless list of personal Brett memories to myself. I've been honored to participate in three different authorship projects involving George and the Royals, and thus had the satisfaction of sharing so many of the good times in print.

Suffice it to say that no one has made me gladder to have stumbled into this profession than this man.

And hearing the words, 'George Brett, Hall of Famer,' no doubt will give me chills to last a lifetime.

For all of that, I can only say: 'Thank you, No. 5.'"
  Steve Cameron, author and first person to interview George in the major leagues

"I've always told George that he was my **favorite five-year-old** in the whole world. I always hoped he'd never grow up, that he'd remain the wonderfully uninhibited, irrepressible man-child whom I've watched celebrate big victories with grilled cheese sandwiches, a few Heinekens, a game of pool and a tape of *Maverick*. I've watched him caddy for his buddy, Larry Ziegler, on the Senior PGA Tour during a baseball lockout. I've watched him buy and wear a Rod Stewart wig so that he would be inconspicuous in New York. I've watched him date a spirited young woman who dipped snuff as easily and casually as he did. But now George is a **husband and a father,** and he seems to be just as skilled at those difficult arts as he was at hitting a 96-mile-an-hour fastball. I guess he isn't my favorite five-year-old anymore, George has grown up. **Now he's my favorite Hall of Famer."**

-Dick Schaap, author and broadcaster

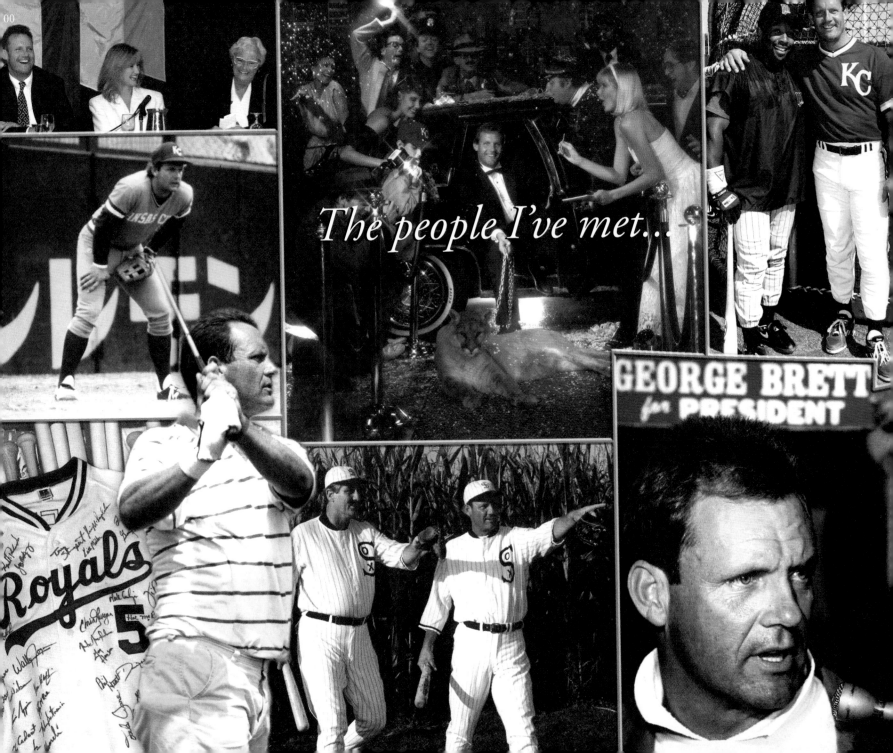

The people I've met...

GEORGE BRETT
for PRESIDENT

Royals
5

The places I've been...

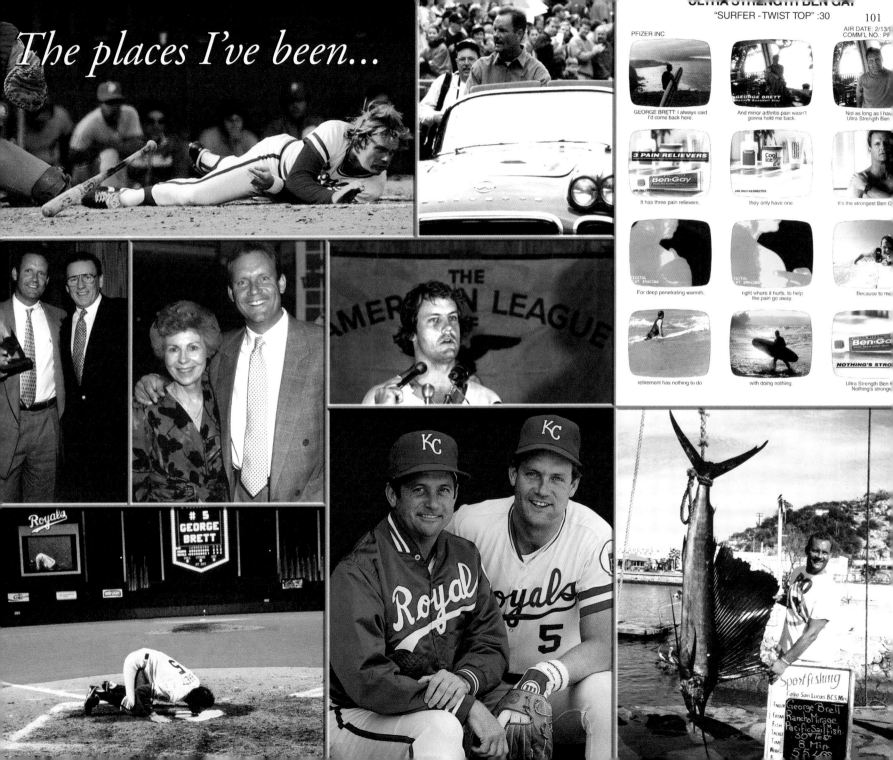

ULTRA STRENGTH BEN GAY
"SURFER - TWIST TOP" :30

PFIZER INC

AIR DATE: 2/13/
COMM'L NO.: PF

GEORGE BRETT: I always said
I'd come back here.

And minor arthritis pain wasn't
gonna hold me back.

Not as long as I hav
Ultra Strength Ben

3 PAIN RELIEVERS

Ben-Gay

It has three pain relievers.

they only have one.

It's the strongest Ben G

For deep penetrating warmth,

right where it hurts, to help
the pain go away.

Because to me

retirement has nothing to do

with doing nothing.

Ultra Strength Ben
Nothing's stronge

NOTHING'S STRO

Ben-Gay

George's thoughts on...

George on his friendship with Rush Limbaugh

Rush and I are still very strong. He didn't get us anything for our wedding-but he did write me a letter. It was the best letter I've ever read in my life. For the wedding present, he said, "Anytime you and Leslie want to go on a honeymoon, you let me know." And this was when he's become mega-successful. "Anywhere you want to go, for as long as you want to go, it's on me." We've never gone on a honeymoon before. I'm afraid to call him up and say, "Rush, we're thinking of going on a honeymoon. We've been married six years, we've got three kids, we'd love to bring our kids with us."

I remember going to New York to play the Yankees. My wife went on that trip with me. We had just gotten married, and Rush was writing his first book, so he was kind of occupied. One time, after his radio show, he said, "Well, I've got some things to do." He asked Leslie if she was going to the game. She said, "Well, I really don't want to." He said, "Why don't you and I go out and have dinner. And then, after the game, George can join us in Manhattan." So they went and had dinner, probably around 9:30-10:00 and I got there about 11:00. We had a great night with him.

I remember once on my birthday, we went out after a Sunday day game. Rush went and Ted (the Famous Chicken) was there. It was kind of fun going to eat chicken with the chicken.

George on the future of the Royals

Whoever owns the Royals isn't going to be a Ewing Kauffman. It's not going to be the same. This town needs somebody, or needs something so we can be competitive again. Now, with a $20-million payroll, it's going to be tough to win. So, is that a problem? Yes, that is a problem.

George on his kids

I hope my kids have the same amount of drive that my brothers and I had as youngsters. To be the best at whatever they want to be. But, to be the best and to work hard to achieve those things. The one thing that I am definitely going to insist upon is that they put forth an effort in their studies. That they try to be good students, not like I was. That's one of my biggest regrets right now. I wish I would have put forth the same effort in my studies as I did in my athletics.

It's our job as parents to be role models. My biggest role model was my father. I had to do things in a way that my father wanted them done, or else we had a discussion about it. I didn't win may discussions with my father.

George on Cooperstown

Friends of mine would come over and we'd talk. They would ask, "What are you going to do this summer?" And I would reply, "I don't know. Hopefully, I'm going to Cooperstown."

It was like the day I retired. I could sit there and think, OK, today I'm here to announce my retirement. I could say it that easily, but once I got there and did it in front of all of those people, it was kind of touchy. OK, I'm in the Hall of Fame. Then I had to go address everybody and it was a moment that I still get a bit choked up about. Hopefully, I'll talk about it enough from now to July 25, so when I stand on those steps, I won't break down like a little baby. What I'm gonna do is I'm gonna call the Hall of Fame and say, "Can you give me some of the other guys' speeches? Give me the guys who cry. Then give me the guys who don't cry."

George on the game

Well, the game has changed, it's really changed. I think it has gotten tougher, not to take away from the guys that played in the 20s, 30s, 40s and 50s. But I really think the game has changed. You've got left-handed long men and right-handed long men. You have left-handed short men and right-handed short men. There were a lot of times in the old days when a guy would go out and throw nine innings regardless of what the score was.

Al Zych, our equipment manager, tells me stories of when he was playing class D. He says, "Yeah, I pitched 12 innings Tuesday and then one of our pitchers got sore and Thursday or Friday I had to come in and pitch 13 innings." They didn't have a relief pitcher. A relief pitcher was a guy who was not good enough to start. Now relief pitchers are born in the minor leagues and in college. You get 2 at-bats, 3 if the guy's throwing a great game, and then you come up in the 7th inning if the game's tight and they bring in a good reliever. Back then, it was you get the same guy, or you'd get a relief pitcher that was not good enough to be a starter.

The older you get, the harder it is. Your body doesn't bounce back the way it did when you were younger. You lose a little quickness.

George on his younger days

I got an autographed ball from Mickey Mantle. It says, "George, I understand you're a lot like I am. You'd better slow down."

I really think that in the 20 years I played, no one had more fun on the field than I did.

George on his brother John

If anybody ever did anything to me, I knew my brother John would get them. After the '77 playoffs, he went to the Yankees locker room, because he had the credentials to get in there, and he heard someone saying, "Brett was on the bottom of the pile and I was kicking him in the head, that s.o.b." Well, he came into our locker room and I'm sitting there with Charley Lau. He wanted to fight every player that walked out of the Yankee locker room. Not only because they beat us, I mean he was upset that they beat us, but because of the things they were saying about me.

To this day, if anybody gives me a tough time, I know he's going to be there for me.

GEORGE BRETT

"NOW HE BELONGS TO THE AGES"

Royals

Royals

Royals

Thanks For The memories #5 BRETT

WRIGLEY FIELD
HOME OF
CHICAGO CUBS
GEORGE BRETT
SIGNS WITH CUBS

QUISENBERRY 29

One thing I'll never forget for the rest of my life: In 1971, when I was leaving to go to Montana, my high school coach and his wife came to the airport, and so did my parents and a lot of my close friends. Here I am, acting like a big, brave, strong warrior going off to war. The troops are leaving, you're saying good-bye to your family. I'm shaking everybody's hand, good luck and things like that. Then I got into that little jetway that goes to the plane and I broke down crying. I was scared to death. It was the first time I'd been on my own in my whole life and I was making $500 a month. Little did I ever know what was in front of me.

Welcome to the Hall of Fame, George Brett.